A SHORTAGE OF GRANDPARENTS

A Memoir of Loss and Discovery

Susan Meier Moss Katz

A SHORTAGE OF GRANDPARENTS
A Memoir of Loss and Discovery

Susan Meier Moss Katz

Copyright © 2017 and 2024
by Susan Meier Moss Katz

Hardcover ISBN 978-1-956381597
Softcover ISBN 978-1-956381603

Mazo Publishers
Website: www.mazopublishers.com
Email: info@mazopublishers.com

54321
All rights reserved.
The text and/or photographs of this book may not be reproduced or translated, stored in a retrieval system, transmitted in any form or by any means, electronic, mechanical, photocopying, recording, used to create derivative works, or otherwise used, without prior permission in writing from the publisher.

...there was a severe shortage of grandparents after the war. Actually, there weren't that many available uncles, aunts, nephews, nieces, or cousins, either.

Thane Rosenbaum
<u>Second Hand Smoke</u>

*This book is dedicated with much gratitude
to my dear friend Dr. Martin Ruch, the
angel from Offenburg who made it
possible
and
in loving memory of
Berthold, Sophie, and Arthur Meier,
who lived these stories.*

The Meier

Berthold's Family

Isaak Dreifuss

Bernhard Meier — Sara Dreifuss Meier 1804 - 1876

David Meier 1844 - 1918

Libkind — Rosa Meier Libkind 1875 -

Sophie Meier Weigel 1876 - — Heinrich Weigel - 1948

Milette Libkind — Raymond Libkind 1909 -

Karl Wiegel

Emil Wiegel

Theodor Libkind 1946 -

Daniel Libkind 1951 -

Barbel Wiegel 1944 -

Wiegel 1946 -

Sophie's Family

Ascher Roland 1780 - 1813 — Sara Levi Roland

Jesia Hahn — Sara Kaufmann Hahn

Isak Roland 1809 - 1876 — Mina Hahn Roland 1813 - 1892

Adolf "Wolf" Roland 1842 - 1896 — Jetta Frank Roland 1850 - 1914

Sophie Roland Meier 1878 - 1942

Roland Family

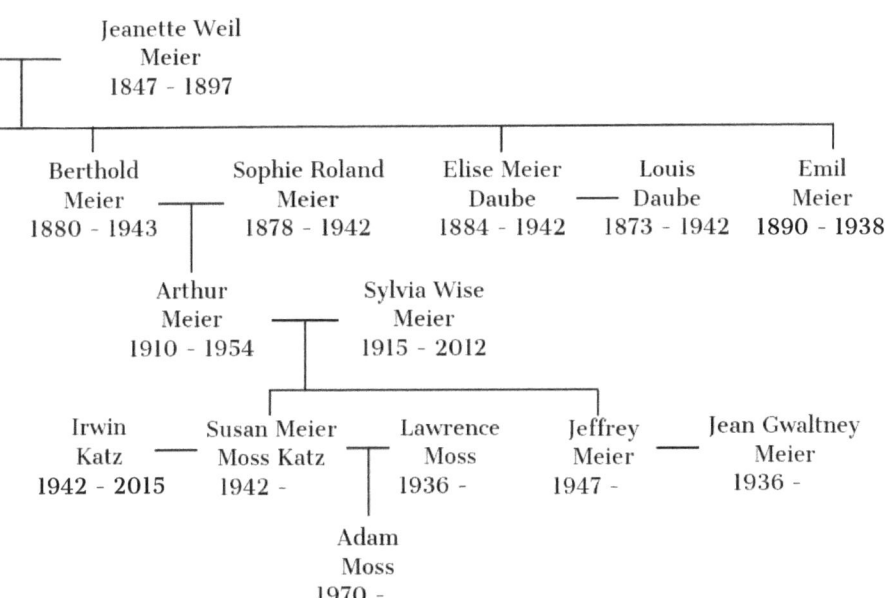

A Note From the Author

I have always loved writing, but I discovered at an early age that writing fiction was not my talent. It was no accident that I was the News Editor of the Reading (PA) High School newspaper. I have always dealt best with facts—who, what, when, where, why?

This book is meant to be a memoir, thus based largely on truth. Writing from my point-of-view, however, meant getting personal, which was hard for me to do, but which liberated me in ways I could never have imagined when I first started writing about the Meier family.

Although the information contained in these pages is true *in spirit,* some of it isn't entirely factual because it can't be entirely factual! Many of these incidents occurred before I was born, and since the stories were told to me second- or even third-hand, I had to write emotional truth. Some things I read in letters, on postcards, or on other documents. In describing them, I had to use my imagination. Even though the stories are almost all true, I wasn't there to witness them happen.

I also had to borrow people's stories, but I could not ask them to elaborate or explain. I often had to invent place and time; sometimes I even had to alter time a bit. I surely had to imagine dialogue and heaven knows, even the people themselves. Most of the people involved are only names to me—sadly, we never met, and we never will.

You will know when I have created a flashback to the past because you will find the chapter has a date and the text is written in italics.

With Martin Ruch's help, I did as much research as was humanly possible. In doing so, I realized that there was history that would not be familiar to most of my readers and which I needed to add to help put the stories in context. In the chapters where I have supplied historical information that is not common knowledge, I have put a border around it to identify that it is background information about the period. A little history lesson, as it were.

Fortunately, I had a treasure trove of real photographs to help me tell the stories. I have put captions to help my readers recognize the main characters. Sadly, I can't give names to a lot of people in the photos as I don't know who many of them are—in some cases even though they may be my relatives. Many of the historical documents included in the book are thanks to Martin.

If you wonder whether this book is autobiographic, I refer you to what the author from whom I borrowed the title for this book—Thane Rosenbaum, the child of Holocaust survivors—said when asked that question. He said that his daughter thinks all of his books are autobiographical. She says every book is really there to recreate a world he didn't see or didn't get a chance to know, things that he wished he could have fixed. Yeah, Thane. Me, too.

Finally, having started writing at such an advanced age, I am under pressure to finish this book because I cannot write forever…time marches on. Before I go, I refuse to allow the Nazis to accomplish their goal of attempting to erase my grandparents' names from history. And so, Dear Reader, here is *A Shortage of Grandparents: A Memoir of Loss and Discovery,* the story of the Meier family, told as honestly as I could tell it.

Susan Meier Moss Katz
Miami, Florida
May 1, 2023

Table of Contents

Dedication
Family Tree
A Note From the Author

Chapter	Title	Page
One	A Shortage of Grandparents	1
Two	Stuttgart, Germany May 1937	7
Three	Travel is Broadening	11
Four	Stolpersteine	15
Five	The Jews of Baden Middle Ages to 1920	17
Six	Living Charmed Lives 1844-1933	25
Seven	What a Difference a War Makes 1933	37
Eight	Leaving a Charmed Life August 1937	43
Nine	A Surprise on the Internet	47
Ten	Serendipity	51
Eleven	The Month from Hell November 1938	55
Twelve	Kristallnacht: Night of Broken Glass November 9-10, 1938	61
Thirteen	Baking Lebkuchen February 1939	69
Fourteen	What They Did Not Get June 1939	71
Fifteen	Starting A New Life	75
Sixteen	The Wagner-Bürckel-Aktion October 21-22, 1940	85

Chapter	Title	Page
Seventeen	Bonbons from Herr Meier October 22, 1940	93
Eighteen	Early Letter from Gurs	95
Nineteen	What's in a Name?	99
Twenty	Pottsville: The Early Years 1941-1947	103
Twenty-One	Pottsville: The House on 22nd Street 1948-1954	113
Twenty-Two	Pottsville: The End 1954	121
Twenty-Three	The Wise Family	129
Twenty-Four	Meeting Helmut Breunig August 1968	139
Twenty-Five	The Little Black Book January 2000	143
Twenty-Six	Serge Klarsfeld: French Nazi-Hunter	147
Twenty-Seven	Go! You Will Find Her! July 16, 2000	149
Twenty-Eight	Camp de Gurs July 18-19, 2000	153
Twenty-Nine	A Visa Too Late January 6, 1943	163
Thirty	Can We Do It Again?	175
Thirty-One	The Green Photo Album	177
Thirty-Two	The Rolands Appear	181
Thirty-Three	Where is Grünstraße 27?	185
Thirty-Four	The Stolpersteine on Grünstraße	191
Thirty-Five	Back to Oberrealschule	199
Thirty-Six	The Stench of Evil	205
Thirty-Seven	Bonbons Redux	211
Thirty-Eight	A Day in Heaven	219

Chapter	Title	Page
Thirty-Nine	Forgiveness	223
Forty	My Fatal Obsession	227
Forty-One	The Hero of the Story	233
Forty-Two	A Tragic Tale	239
Forty-Three	An Unfortunate Coincidence	247
Forty-Four	How Was the Play, Mrs. Lincoln?	249
	Epilogue	257
	Acknowledgements	259
	Sources	271
	About the Author	275

Chapter One

A Shortage of Grandparents

In the poignant 2017 Argentinian/Spanish film written and directed by Pablo Solarz, *"The Last Suit,"* the main character, a Polish Holocaust survivor with numbers tattooed on his arm, explains how his parents and sister died in the Holocaust. "I wasn't told about it. I saw it all," he says several times.

That's not how it happened for me. I didn't see it. I was told about it. As far back as I can remember, I listened to stories about how my grandparents died in the Holocaust.

And, you might ask, how did you deal with what you heard? Well, to tell the embarrassing truth, I spent nearly a lifetime perfecting my skills of avoidance. I worked very hard at trying to prevent learning the truth of how and why my grandparents, my father's German parents, died. And why my father died so young—March 8, 2023 was the 69th anniversary of his death. I didn't have much information, and I was too afraid to look for more. For the first 60 years of my life, I was the *Queen of Fear* who lived in the *Cave of Avoidance*.

The Holocaust ended in 1945. At least that's what the history books say. That is not necessarily a fact. For some of us, it never ended. The Holocaust cast a long shadow over the survivors, their children, and their grandchildren. It still does.

I am now 80 years old and have children and grandchildren of my own. I was born in Pottsville, Pennsylvania on December 24, 1942. I was the lucky generation that had the good fortune to be born in America. I never saw the nightmare that went on in Germany in the 1930s and 1940s. I only heard about it. And pretended I didn't.

Because my grandparents were dead, I thought they held no place in my life. They were just pictures among many nameless people in a green photo album and the authors of a pile of tissue-thin, yellowing letters and old postcards, all written in German, that sat in a box, unopened and never translated. Oh, and they were also the original owners of some beautiful pieces of silver

Chapter One

and table linens monogrammed with *SR* for Sophie Roland or *BM* for Berthold Meier which my mother used on holidays. These things were just artifacts, and so I didn't have to deal with what they meant and where they came from. How naïve of me—I had no idea how much influence Sophie and Berthold Meier were having on me even though I was ignoring them.

As a child, I didn't even know that my German father was different from my friends' fathers. One day in elementary school, one of the kids in my classroom taunted me by telling me that my father "talked funny." I went home crying, asking my mother for consolation. She calmed me down and then told me what I had somehow missed—my father did "talk funny." He had a German accent. I had no idea!

Because I did not grow up in a house with a survivor of the Holocaust as some children did, I did not live with the consequences that would have meant. My father left Germany in 1937 and had no numbers tattooed on his arm. Except for his passion for music and his relationship with his German treasures stored on the third floor of our house, he seemed just like everybody else's father. His love of athletics made the transition to American baseball easier—he played it, and he loved listening to it on the radio. All I knew was that his parents had died in the Holocaust.

What I did not realize was that their mysterious deaths unconsciously haunted me from the moment I was born.

From childhood on I now realize, I felt as though I escaped death only by being born a generation too late. I unconsciously believed that only good fortune kept me from being a witness to or a victim of the horrors that the Nazis brought to my family. And the world seemed like a very unsafe place where the Holocaust could happen again. That's where the real root of my fear lay. I don't suppose that has ever changed, even now.

The only lasting positive impression I had of Germany was my father's frequent description of the people in his hometown—Gengenbach—as *good* people. And that he dearly missed his best friend, Helmut Breunig. I was far too young to have known enough to ask my father about how his life changed when the

Nazis came to power or what life was like when he finally got to America. I was only 11 years old when my father died—whether or not he would ever have told me about his experiences in Germany from 1933 to 1937 and about how he felt about the fate of his parents, I will never know. The few contemporaries I have whose parents lived through the Holocaust often could not get them, even in old age, to talk about their experiences—their memories were too painful for them to discuss.

The only person I ever met from Gengenbach during my childhood was my father's friend, Franz Blum, who moved to Argentina with his family before my father came to America. Franz traveled to the United States regularly, and so he was the only consistent link I had to Germany. He remained a part of my life for fifty years, but I never asked him enough questions. After my father died, it was important and special for me to have Franz as a connection to my father and Gengenbach. By the time I was looking for the information he could have supplied, he had died of old age.

Franz Blum encouraged me to make a trip to Gengenbach in 1968 with my first husband, Lawrie. I traveled there like a tourist—I didn't ask any questions about the Holocaust or about my grandparents. I could have—the people I met, like Helmut Breunig, knew a lot more about the fates of Sophie and Berthold Meier than I did. I was thrilled to be seeing where my family came from. I just looked around when I was invited by Karl Lambrecht and his wife to come into the Meier family house on Grünstraße, even though I knew that the man who was showing me around had *bought* the house from my grandparents for a pittance after Jews had been forced to sell their property in 1939, and, I suspected, even in my avoidance, that some of the furniture I was seeing probably once belonged to the Meier family. Lambrecht even showed me the view of the town from the bay window, a view several generations of my family had seen each day.

Chapter One

View from the bay window

Adolf and Elfriede Lohmüller and Susan Meier Moss, in front of the house with the Lambrechts

I kept my mouth shut for the whole week Lawrie and I spent in Gengenbach, guided throughout by Adolf and Elfriede Lohmüller, our guides from the town, carefully avoiding hearing any truths. Instead, I drank a lot of local German wine—one special bottle in the garden of the Mayor, Herr Schrempp, a schoolmate of my father's—and I smiled a lot.

By the time, I got around to wanting to ask questions and hear the answers, Helmut Breunig and Karl Lambrecht were both dead. I later learned that the agreement Lambrecht had made with Berthold and Sophie Meier was that they were supposed to be allowed to live in the house with him and his family after they sold it to him, but that my grandparents felt so unsafe that they quickly moved out. I also learned that the money from the sale of the house was stolen by the Nazis when they sent my grandparents to Camp de Gurs. By the time I found these things out, there was no one to discuss these ugly revelations with.

I compulsively avoided books and movies about the Holocaust because they made me too sad and too angry, and, I also believe now, they evoked survivor's guilt in me. How could this happen to *my* grandparents? I felt tremendous rage whenever I came across pictures of the victims of the death camps. The Seventh Grade Holocaust class was held on Monday nights in my classroom at Beth Am Day School in Miami where I taught for 22 years. The Holocaust teacher was given one bulletin board in my room on which to hang his educational material. I made the school install window shades that I could keep down and he could pull up for class to uncover his posters of Auschwitz and other horrors each Monday night! I justified my request by saying that it was because I didn't want the kids in my class to see the pictures depicted on the posters. The truth is, I didn't want to see the pictures depicted on the posters.

My anxiety was so great that during a trip to Israel in 1985, when the group I was with went to Yad Vashem, the Holocaust Museum in Jerusalem, I insisted on doing my own tour, alone. I had no way of knowing whether or not I would find myself discovering pictures of my grandparents, and if that happened, I wanted to be by myself. I was looking FOR pictures—not AT

Chapter One

them—as most of the tour members were. I also didn't want anyone to see the pain and rage I felt as I walked through that museum. When we all met up at the end, I felt relieved. It was over and I had seen no pictures of my family nor embarrassed myself by freaking out in front of anyone else. Truthfully, the rest of the group was probably as seriously shaken as I was.

And so, the *Queen of Fear* lived successfully in her *Cave of Avoidance* for 60 years.

Chapter Two

Stuttgart, Germany

May 1937

Arthur Meier opened the heavy brown wooden door and saw a room filled with people, all crowded into a place meant to hold only a few at a time. The hard brown wooden chairs were all occupied, mainly by the oldest people in the room. The rest of the men and women leaned against empty places on the walls. A few younger people even sat on the floor. Arthur edged his way into the room and was able to find a place to stand against a wall, thanks to a man who looked to be about his age and who moved over to make room for him. There were two large desks at the back of the room, at which were seated two men. As they called out a name, the designated person left his or her place against the wall or chair and walked over to one of the desks.

Some of the transactions took only a few moments; others took longer. A few of the people turned away from the desks looking happy, but most left with a look of frustration or anger on their faces. A few even left crying.

It was May 1937 and Arthur was at the American Consulate in Stuttgart where visas were obtained for travel out of Germany to America. It was the nearest place to his hometown, Gengenbach, for him to get a visa to go to the United States. By now, he was familiar with this office since it was his sixth visit in four years. He prayed it would be his last. He hoped that this time his place in the quota list would come up so that he could finally book a ticket on a ship leaving France in the near future. Life in Germany had become intolerable for Jews. Arthur was only twenty-six years old—his entire future still lay in front of him. He knew it couldn't and shouldn't be spent in Germany...

He knew from his previous visits that this wait could be several hours long. He had brought a leather bag with a book to read and some fruit and cheese in case he got hungry. Most of the

Chapter Two

people waiting had also brought food with them, and many of them were munching on something. Arthur guessed that they had learned from earlier visits to this place that a long wait was inevitable.

The man who had made room for him was now leaning against the wall with his eyes closed. He appeared to be dozing, another way to pass the endless wait. After about a half hour, he woke up, and, reaching into his bag, pulled out an apple and began to eat it. He looked at Arthur and introduced himself, "Hello, I'm Herman Bodenheimer."

"I'm Arthur Meier. From Gengenbach."

"I'm from Durbach," Herman said. "We're practically neighbors." They both laughed.

"And how many visits to this splendid place have you made?" Arthur asked sarcastically.

"This is my sixth visit. And hopefully my last."

"Ah, the same as me. I've been here that much, too. Where are you hoping to go in the United States?"

"I've got a cousin in the United States who is sponsoring me," Herman answered. "My cousin Emanuel."

"Me, too. My Uncle Emil, my father's brother, lives there already."

"Where?" Herman asked, this time taking a pear out of his cloth bag and beginning to eat.

"Eastern Pennsylvania," Arthur explained. "From the pictures my uncle sent me it looks like Germany."

"That's funny," Herman exclaimed, looking surprised. "I'm going to Pennsylvania, too. My cousin sells wholesale hardware and has offered me a job. What a small world! Where in Pennsylvania are you going?"

"A place called Reading."

Herman Bodenheimer's jaw dropped open, and his green eyes practically popped out of his head. "Oh, my God!" he spluttered, spitting pieces of pear out of his mouth as he spoke. "I'm going to Reading, Pennsylvania too!"

The two men stared at each other in complete astonishment, speechless. They both began to laugh at the same time.

Just then Herman's name was called by one of the clerks. "I'll be back," he assured Arthur as he walked away. Arthur watched Herman and could tell by the smile on his face that his visa application was finally approved. After he was finished with the consulate people, Herman walked back to him. They talked for a few minutes and then Arthur's name was called.

"I'll wait here for you," Herman called to him as Arthur walked toward the back of the room.

With relief, Arthur was told that he also was finally approved for a visa. That meant that at long last, he could buy a ticket on a ship leaving for New York and leave Germany behind. Now he could get on a train and go to Paris to stay with his Aunt Rosa until the ship sailed. Leaving his parents behind was something he had been trying to deal with for four years. There was nothing he could do except try to get them out of Germany as soon as possible once he was settled in America. Hopefully, that wouldn't take as long as it had taken him to get his visa.

Arthur walked back to Herman and the men shook hands in mutual happiness.

"Where are you going now?" Herman asked.

"I'll take the first train I can get to Offenburg," Arthur said. "Then I'll catch the next local to Gengenbach. Are you going home, too?"

"I am," Herman assured him. "We can ride together as far as Offenburg."

The two young German Jewish men rode to Offenburg together and then said their goodbyes. Arthur waited for the next train home.

Herman Bodenheimer and Arthur Meier remained friends in Pennsylvania until Arthur died in 1954. Whenever the two men saw each other, they always appreciated how good it felt to see a familiar face in the strange and foreign place they had escaped to and how small the world really is.

Chapter Three

Travel is Broadening

It was May 11, 2017 and I was on a Jewish tour in the town of Regensburg, Germany. We had a lovely young Viking River Cruise tour guide for the morning, very knowledgeable about her subject. In my research before the cruise, I had read that on the Regensburg Cathedral, on the wall that faced what had once been the Jewish Quarter of the town—almost every German City had what once was the Jewish Quarter—there was a relief of a pig with three Jews nursing from her nipples. Sure enough, the odious plaque was right where it was supposed to be. No one in the group except me seemed particularly interested in it. Having seen such anti-Semitic reliefs on churches in Provence, France on my trip there in 2000 with Irwin, I was not surprised at this early symbol of the anti-Semitic depiction of the Jew in European society. Just disgusted and sad at this reminder of how old hatred of the Jews really is.

Next, the guide took us to the ruins of the synagogue—another constant in Europe—visiting where the synagogue used to be.

It was just past there that I saw them—the Regensburg *Stolpersteine*.

And why, you might be wondering, was I on a Jewish tour in Regensburg, Germany on a Viking River Cruise in May of 2017? Let me tell you.

My dear husband Irwin died on May 3, 2015 in Chania, Crete during a cruise to the Greek Islands. He hadn't planned to die on that vacation. But he did. I hadn't planned on it either. Bringing my husband's dead body home to Miami on a series of flights that took a week was not in my plans either. Neither was writing his obituary for the Miami Herald in the lobby of a hotel in Athens, Greece nor was delivering a eulogy for a 72-year-old man I adored at the end of that long week when his body and I got back to Miami.

It took me over a year to recover from the shock of Irwin's

Chapter Three

sudden and unexpected death and the settling of his affairs. Once things calmed down, I found that I was left with a broken heart and a missing identity. And lots of time on my hands. I knew I had to find something to do with myself. If I hadn't retired from my job as a school administrator two years earlier, I would never have had this dilemma. When I worked, which I did as an educator for over fifty years, I could barely find time to breathe. But, I wasn't an educator anymore, and I wasn't a wife anymore, and I wasn't finding things to do except crying to fill my time anymore. And at night, when I couldn't sleep, eating... eating everything in my house that wasn't crawling.

About a year after Irwin died, friends of mine asked me if I wanted to join them on a Viking River Cruise from Budapest to Amsterdam the following May. It sounded like a good idea for many reasons. They were old friends—I wouldn't feel strange with them. At least, I didn't think I'd feel strange. After all, they were my friends long before I met Irwin. They had been my friends in my first marriage and had stuck by my side when that ended after 25 years. And going on a river cruise felt safe. My husband had died while we were on an ocean cruise, so I had crossed ocean cruises off my list. Forever. But the Danube River Cruise seemed harmless. And by then, Irwin would be gone for two years, surely time for me to start traveling again. Besides, I hadn't been to Germany, my father's birthplace, since Lawrie and I had visited my father's town of Gengenbach almost 50 years earlier.

So, I said, "Yes! I'll go on the river cruise with you." And that was how it happened that I was in Regensburg, Germany in 2017.

For a first-time solo traveler, I was really brave. I even flew to Budapest two days before my friends arrived for the cruise. Months before the trip, I arranged for a lovely Jewish woman named Anni to be my guide. She picked me up at the airport and drove me to my hotel. I stayed at a Hilton Hotel on the beautiful Buda side of the Danube. Each night I ate dinner by myself at small Hungarian restaurants within walking distance of the hotel. The waiters and waitresses were very helpful and even spoke some English. They helped me order, and I ate good Hungarian food. Each morning Anni picked me up and off we went. It was like traveling with a friend.

For two days, she showed me all of beautiful Budapest and even the charming little village of Szentendre, outside Budapest, where her family came from. We talked nonstop—exchanging life stories as we drove around the city. The traffic in Budapest is so bad that we had plenty of time to get to know each other. At the end of the second day, Anni dropped me and my luggage off at the ship, and we said goodbye. I felt very sorry to see her go—I wished she were coming on the ship with me.

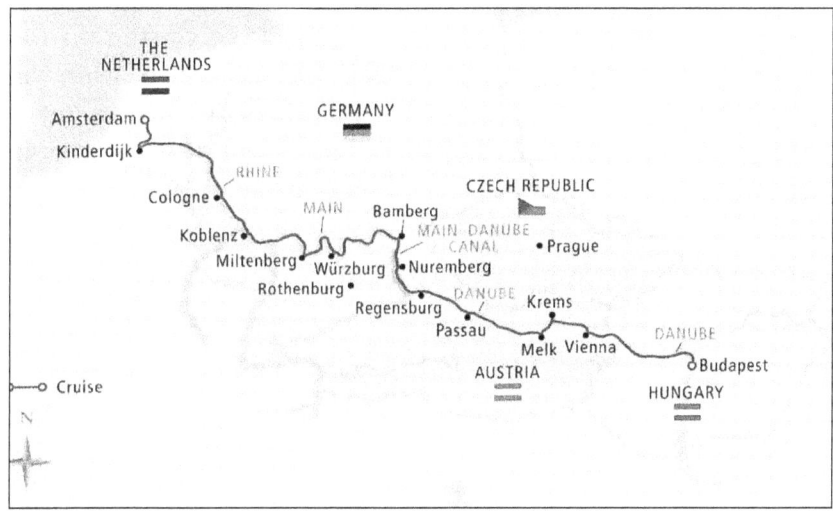

The route of the Viking Cruise ship from Budapest, Hungary to Amsterdam, the Netherlands

After I checked in at the desk, I went to find my travel companions. It was easy—they were next door to me. The ship was so much smaller than a cruise ship that getting around was very simple. There weren't too many places to get lost on that tiny boat.

The river cruise began in Budapest, on the Danube River, then went to Vienna, and from there it traveled into Germany, moving to the Rhine River. Every day there was a new port. If you liked a place, tough luck! It was a visit to a sight and then right back to the ship—no different from ocean cruising but just on a smaller ship and with fewer people. That is cruising. The reason people

Chapter Three

like cruising is because they don't have to keep packing and unpacking. And the fact that "it's Tuesday so it must be Vienna" works just fine for them. Plus, you can eat and drink yourself to death.

That was not how Irwin and I liked to travel. We liked flying to places, renting a car and driving, taking our time, and stopping if we saw something interesting. But I sure wasn't doing that anymore—alone. So, here I was, on a river cruise, out of my comfort zone but managing to keep my discomfort to myself. At least the things we were seeing, however briefly, were very interesting and often beautiful.

I had signed up for tours months before we started on the cruise. In several places, Jewish tours were offered. Given the fact that I was descended from a long line of German Jews, I had naturally signed up for all of them. The first one was in Regensburg, Germany. I had no idea that my life was about to change forever that day.

Chapter Four

Stolpersteine

I looked down and saw some brass plaques embedded in the sidewalk. Looking closer, I saw that they each started with a person's name and that the final entry on each one was the name of a concentration camp. I grabbed the Viking Cruise guide's arm and asked her what these brass plaques were.

"These are *Stolpersteine*," said the young woman, pointing down at the five small brass markers on the Regensburg sidewalk. "They were put here in memory of the Jews who once lived in this house and who were taken to concentration camps where they died."

I looked down at the markers again and read the name on each one...Joseph Lilienfeld, Paul Lilienfeld, Ida Lilienfeld, Erich Herrscher, Alma Herrscher...and then I noticed that they also told the date of each person's death.

The first Stolpersteine I ever saw were in the Jewish Quarter in Regensburg, Germany

Chapter Four

My heart began to beat very fast. "Who put them here?" I asked excitedly, trying not to shout.

"Gunter Demnig—the man who started the *Stolpersteine* project. *Stolpersteine* means *stumbling stone*. Demnig started the project a number of years ago in Germany but now it's all over Europe—in all the countries where the Nazis took Jews from their homes during the Holocaust," the guide said.

I took out my phone and began to take pictures of the Regensburg *Stolpersteine*. Then I looked down at them again, and in my mind, imagined two new shiny brass markers—*"Berthold Meier, Sophie Meier"*—in front of 27 Grünstraße, my grandparents' home in Gengenbach. "My grandparents died in the Holocaust," I said to the guide. "They lived in a small town in Baden."

I could see on her face that she understood what I was feeling. "You can write down the information," she offered in a very helpful way. "It takes about two years, but you can contact Demnig and get started." She tore a piece of paper out of her notebook, and I wrote *Stolpersteine – Gunter Demnig*.

Carefully, I folded and tucked the slip of paper into a pocket in my wallet. "Thank you," I said, smiling at her.

Chapter Five

The Jews of Baden

Middle Ages to 1920

Anti-Semitism was alive and well in Europe and the rest of the world throughout history, with Jews regularly expelled from places they lived in, for many reasons. History shows that although Germany as a whole was not known as a particularly welcoming place for Jews, one of the few places where Jewish people were given some early form of protection was in the Grand Duchy of Baden.

The Grand Duchy of Baden, Germany

Baden is in the southwestern part of Germany, tucked between France and Switzerland and bordered by the Rhine River and Lake Constance.

Chapter Five

Examining the history of Baden reveals why some Jews choose to live in this part of Germany very far back in time, including my ancestors—the Meier and Roland families—who settled in the State of Baden as early as the 1800's or perhaps even earlier.

Meier family members lived in the cities of Diersburg, Lahr, and finally, Gengenbach, a city settled in by Jews as early as the Middle Ages. This beautiful village is where David Meier bought the house on Grünstraße in 1881.

Sinsheim, a little farther north in Baden, near Heidelberg, also had Jewish residents as early as the 13th century. This was where Sophie Roland Meier's family had lived since at least the 1800's. The Jewish Cemetery in Sinsheim is filled with a number of graves of members of the Roland family.

What made Baden so welcoming was that here Jews were allowed to engage in commerce, moneylending, livestock trading and retail trading. In the first constitutional edict of May 14, 1807 in Baden, Judaism was recognized as a tolerated religion, and its members were considered "Schutzjuden," "protected Jews." Soon, the Jews of Baden began to get local civil rights, with requirements often imposed by the state. In 1809, for example, they were required to adopt permanent family names, something Jews had not customarily done. These early rights and economic opportunities in Baden could very well explain why the Meier and Roland families settled there so early in time. Baden Jewry was also one of the earliest German Jewish Territorial Organizations to establish a state-recognized central organization, the "Oberrat," or "Supreme Council," to represent the affairs of the community. However, when the Reform Movement began in the early 19th century, German Jews began to break into two separate groups.

In the years before and after WWI, there was a gradual transformation of the German Jewish population that made them appear to fit in with the rest of Germany's citizens. One major cause was the drop in the Jewish birthrate, making Jews stand out less in the general population of Germany. In 1862, there were 24,099 Jews living in Baden. By 1933, that number had dropped to 20,617. That was true for the declining population of Jews all over Germany.

Jews began to blend into German society by embracing German literature, philosophy, and music. Another way their Jewish distinctness began to mellow was that Jewish students began to attend schools in the German educational system, rather than the traditional Jewish schools they had once attended. Arthur Meier, who was born in 1910, was a perfect example of all these changes occurring in German Jews born in the 20th Century.

A combination of a relaxing of the observance of Orthodox customs and the use of the Yiddish language, combined with the birth of Reform Judaism, which adopted many Protestant features, further helped to make the German Jews appear more like the rest of the population. One important fact to remember about the Jews of Germany, however, is that they were considered politically moderate, originally a positive quality, but one which will rear its ugly head later in time when the Nazis would use it against them.

At the same time that Jews were beginning to fit into German society, there were some other forces that offset this positive perception, continuing to make them stand out and appear different, more prosperous, and therefore, intimidating. Many Jews made their living in the occupations of trade and commerce, which made them become identified as a non-manual labor force. In addition, Jews were three times more likely to own their own businesses than the average German worker. Fifteen percent of the lawyers in Germany were Jews and six percent were doctors and dentists, again in contrast to the average German. Prosperity was good for the Jewish population but was surely resented by many Germans. "As rich as a Rothschild" was a commonly used trope symbolizing the view of the wealth of Jews in Germany and in the rest of Europe.

European alliances and rivalries had been causing tension throughout Europe for many years prior to World War I, particularly in the Balkan region of southeast Europe, mainly Serbia, which was supported by Russia and France, against the Austria-Hungarian Empire, which was supported by Germany. Germany desperately wanted a war with Russia to break up the French-Russian alliance.

Chapter Five

While the main causes of World War I were militarism, secret alliances, imperialism, and nationalistic pride, there was one single event, the assassination of Archduke Franz Ferdinand of Austria and his wife, by a Serbian nationalist in Sarajevo in 1914, that set off the chain of events leading to World War I, also known as "The Great War." Germany gave Austria-Hungary "carte blanche" support, and on July 28, 1914, Austria-Hungary declared war on Serbia, beginning a war that lasted until 1918. Germany, Austria-Hungary, Bulgaria, and the Ottoman Empire, called the Central Powers, fought against Great Britain, France, Russia, Italy, Romania, Canada, Japan, and the United States, called the Allied Powers.

World War I was the bloodiest conflict the world had ever seen thanks to new military technologies and the horrors of trench warfare. By the time it was over, and the Allied Powers claimed victory, more than 16 million people—soldiers and civilians alike—were dead.

Many young Jewish men were conscripted as soldiers to serve in the Germany Army in World War I, including Berthold Meier from Gengenbach.

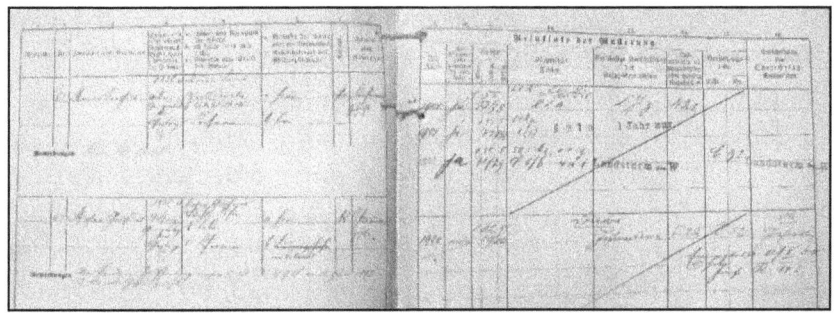

These pictures show my grandfather, Berthold Meier, a Landsturm soldier in World War I and a copy of his actual Army record from his years of service in the German Army

The "Treaty of Versailles," signed in Paris in June 1919, forced Germany and the other Central Powers to take all the blame for World War I. This meant a loss of territories, reduction in military forces, and reparation payments to the Allied Powers. The "Treaty of Versailles" reduced Germany's European territory by roughly 13% and stripped the country of all its overseas territories and colonies. The German Army was to be limited to 100,000 men, and all German soldiers had to be volunteers. Germany was not allowed to have armored vehicles, submarines, or aircraft, and the German Navy could build only six battleships. The Rhineland became a demilitarized zone.

Perhaps the most humiliating part of the treaty for the defeated Germans was Article 231, commonly known as the "War Guilt Clause." This clause forced the German nation to accept complete responsibility for starting the war.

Vengeance became the winner in the writing of the "Treaty of Versailles." While England did not want to exact the revenge that ended up being imposed, most of the other victors did. Originally, American President Woodrow Wilson did not intend to support those who demanded that Germany be forced to pay such a heavy price for its defeat, but after arriving in Paris for the negotiations, he came down with the Spanish Flu. Apparently recovered, but behaving erratically, he went along with the harsher terms demanded by a number of the other countries. In the end, those seeking vengeance against Germany prevailed

Chapter Five

and it was held liable for all material damages from the war. The "Treaty of Versailles" had an immediate, long-lasting, and crippling effect on the German economy.

Converting to a peacetime economy in Germany was made even more difficult because of rising unemployment and rising inflation. Soon, the German currency was not worth the paper it was printed on—people were seen pushing wheelbarrows of money to the stores. On October 27, 1923, an article in the newspaper of Gengenbach stated that the city would print emergency money notes with amounts between one million and one billion marks to deal with the devalued currency.

This 500 million Mark was one of the emergency money notes printed by the city of Gengenbach

The price of losing the war that the winners would exact from the German government and the German people would become the beginning of events no one could foresee in 1918. It would unleash the forces that would allow Adolf Hitler to become Chancellor of Germany only fifteen years later—a defeat so costly that it would very quickly lead to the Holocaust and to World War II.

Gengenbach had to tell its citizens how to treat the soldiers returning from the war:

Der Kinzig-Bote. Gengenbacher Wochenblatt. 28. September 1919:
Unsere Stadt hat zum Empfang der Kriegsgefangenen, welche nächster Tage zurückkehren werden, Festschmuck angelegt. Letzter Tage sind schon einige Gefangene wohlbehalten hier eingetroffen; weitere werden in nächster Zeit erwartet

The Kinzig Messenger, Gengenbacher Weekly, September 28, 1919:
Our city has put on festive decorations for the reception of the prisoners of war, who will return next days. Some prisoners have arrived here safely in the last days; more are expected in the near future.

Offenburg, 7. Januar 1920:
Es ist umgehend zu berichten: Zahl der zurückgekehrten Kriegsgefangenen (25), Zahl der noch zu erwartenden Kriegsgefangenen (23).

Offenburg, January 7, 1920:
It must be reported immediately: Number of returned prisoners of war (25), number of prisoners of war still to be expected (23).

Der Kinzig-Bote, 27. Januar 1920:
Die Kriegsgefangenen, die jetzt aus der französischen Gewalt in die Heimat entlassen werden, haben besonders Schweres mitgemacht. Es dürfte deshalb die Bitte berechtigt sein, die Heimat möchte den zurückkehrenden Söhnen allen, ohne Ausnahme, einen recht herzlichen Empfang bereiten. Wenn wir den Heimkehrenden zeigen, dass wir sie trotz des Unglücks des Vaterlandes nicht vergessen haben, so werden sie gerne bereit sein, mit uns zu arbeiten an dem Wiederaufbau unserer deutschen Heimat. – Am letzten Freitag ist der erste, seit 5 Jahren in französischer Gefangenschaft sich befindende Josef Göppert von Strohbach aus dem Gefangenenlager zurückgekehrt. Hoffentlich folgend die übrigen Gefangenen bald nach.

The Kinzig Messenger, 27 January 1920:
The prisoners of war, who are now being released from the French violence into their homeland, have undergone particularly difficult circumstances. It may therefore be justified to ask the homeland to give a very warm welcome to all, without exception, the returning sons. If we show the homecomers that we have not forgotten them despite the misfortune of our homeland, they will be happy to work with us on the reconstruction of our German homeland. - Last Friday, Josef Göppert von Strohbach, who has been in French captivity for 5 years, returned from the prison camp. Hopefully the remaining prisoners will follow soon after.

Gengenbach, 20. März 1920:
Bürgermeister an den Gesangverein Gngenbach: Die Gemeinde beabsichtigt am Sonntag, den 18. April dieses Jahres, nachdem nunmehr auch die sämtlichen Kriegsgefangenen zurückgekehrt sind, eine Feier für die heimgekehrten Krieger zu veranstalten. Zur Verschönerung der Feier ist gewünscht worden, dass sich hieran auch die hiesigen Gesangsvereine beteiligen und durch ihren Gesang zur würdigen Feier des Tages beitragen. Indem wir Ihnen hiervon Nachricht geben, bitten wir hierzu Stellung nehmen zu wollen und uns das Ergebnis bald mitteilen zu wollen.
Der Bürgermeister

Gengenbach, March 20, 1920:
The Mayor to the Gengenbach Singing Society: On Sunday, April 18 of this year, after all the prisoners of war have returned, the community intends to organize a celebration for the warriors who have returned home. For the embellishment of the celebration, it was wished that the local choral societies also take part in it and contribute by their singing to the worthy celebration of the day. By informing you of this, we ask you to comment on this and to inform us of the result as soon as possible.

The Mayor

Chapter Five

Throughout history, the Jews, with their economic success and their use of strange and untraditional customs and languages, had been traditional targets, easily blamed for disease, economic downturns, and for misfortunes besetting various peoples and nations. After the defeat of Germany in World War I, even though many German Jewish men served as soldiers in the war, history would tragically repeat itself again.

When Germany lost the war, all of the contributions that Jews had made as German citizens were quickly forgotten. In <u>Mein Kampf</u>, Hitler claimed that Germany would have won World War I if there had been more Jewish soldiers, implying that too few Jews acted like loyal Germans.

Kaiser Wilhelm also blamed the Jews for Germany's loss of the war and declared to the world that an international Jewish conspiracy controlled all the forces against Germany. The incidence of violent acts on Jews began to become more common. These problems led to extremist positions with simplified explanations, much of them directed against the Jews.

World War I is often referred to as "The War to End All Wars." Perhaps a better name would be "The War That Began the Holocaust."

Chapter Six

Living Charmed Lives

1844-1933

A baby named David was born to Bernhard Meier, a merchant, and Sara Meier, née Dreifuss, his wife, on June 29, 1844 at 6 AM in the town of Diersburg, Germany. The birth was recorded in the Book of Birth of the town, with Marx Oppenheimer and Salomon Weil, both merchants from Diersburg, witnessing the entry.

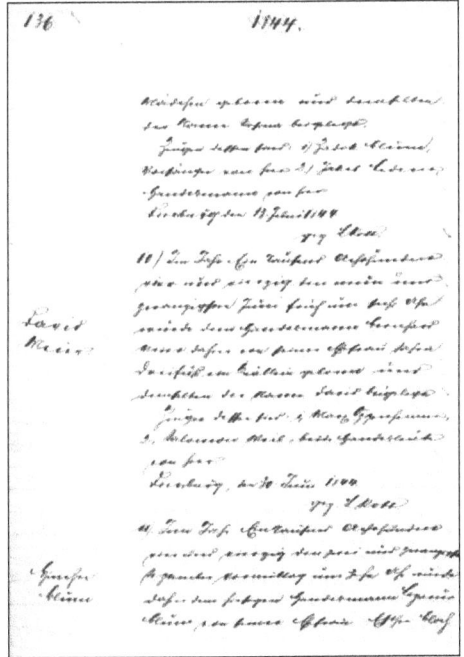

A copy of the actual page from the Book of Birth of Diersburg, Germany showing David Meier's birth on June 29, 1844

David Meier grew up, took over his father's tobacco business, and married Jeanette Weil from Lahr.

Chapter Six

David Meier

Jeanette Weil Meier

The couple had five children: Rosa, Sophie (May 28, 1876), Berthold (March 9, 1880), Elise (January 1, 1884) and Emil (October 9, 1890). On April 27, 1881, David Meier bought a house, 27 Grünstraße, in Gengenbach, a charming old town in the southern Black Forest of Germany and moved his family and his business there.

The house on Grünstraße sat between the Kinzig River and the railway line that ran through the town and had a lovely garden filled with colorful flowering plants and wonderful pear trees. Sadly, Jeanette Meier died at age 49 on June 1, 1897.

David Meier's oldest son, Berthold, married Sophie Roland, from Sinsheim, in 1909. Their son, Arthur, was born on July 24, 1910. Berthold moved his wife and their child into the house with his father on Grünstraße.

The Meier family were Orthodox Jews who kept a kosher home. They got their meat from a local butcher who observed the Jewish ritual for slaughtering animals. Occasionally, they ordered special foods from the kosher butcher in Strasbourg, a French city just across the Rhine River from Gengenbach. Arthur's mother Sophie came from a family of Reform Jews, but after her marriage to Berthold in 1909, Sophie learned the customs of keeping a kosher home.

Berthold and Sophie Meier with their young son Arthur in front of the house on Grünstraße in about 1911. The maids with their heads looking out of the windows and the gardener tending the pear trees are also seen in the picture

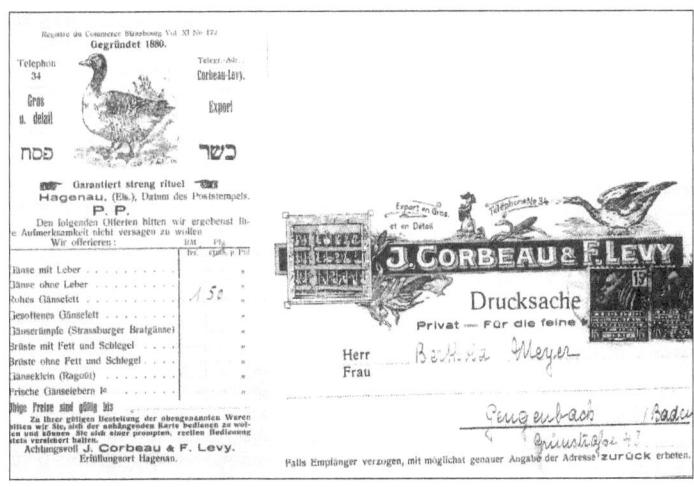

The back and front of a postcard from a kosher butcher for goose fat, used for making paté. In Hebrew it says that the order was kosher for Passover

Chapter Six

Tobacco wholesaling had been the business of the Meier family going back many generations. In each generation, the oldest son of the Meier family learned the business from his father and continued what was a successful and established company. In the beginning, the Meier men traveled by horse and wagon around the towns in the area of the southern Black Forest. Later, they began to ride the train, and, eventually, their travels were made by car.

This postcard from 1922 was sent to the firm of David Meier, Cigar Store, in Gengenbach

Berthold Meier took over the tobacco business from his father, David. Arthur Meier, too, was expected to take over the business from his father, Berthold, when he finished his education.

For the first twenty-three years of his life, Arthur Meier lived a charmed existence. He grew up living in the beautiful house on Grünstraße with his mother Sophie, his father Berthold, his grandfather, David, a widower, and his dog, Feldmann.

Arthur as a little boy   As a schoolboy   Arthur and his mother Sophie

When Arthur was five years old, Germany entered World War I. His father was conscripted into a unit of Landsturm soldiers, a regional militia of older, untrained German soldiers, and was sent off to fight in France.

Berthold Meier is seated third from the left in the front row of his Landstrum militia group

Berthold was captured and spent the next five years in a French prisoner-of-war camp. David Meier and his son Berthold never saw each other again. On March 20, 1918, while Berthold was a prisoner of the French, and when Arthur was eight years old, David, who had lived to be 73 years old, died and was buried in the Jewish Cemetery in Offenburg.

Berthold took over the tobacco business when he returned home from France in 1920 after the Allies freed the German prisoners, but he had to deal with the consequences of Germany's defeat and humiliation at the hands of the winning Allied Forces which greatly depressed the German economy after the war.

Arthur went to elementary school with many friends from his town, children he had known his whole life. There were only two other Jews in his class, so most of the 34 children in the class were Catholic or Protestant. The Jewish children were accepted by the other students, only occasionally getting a friendly teasing about "smelling like garlic," an insult commonly made to Jews.

Chapter Six

Arthur Meier is seated in the center of the second row from the front, wearing the white sailor collar, and seated directly to his right is Helmut Breunig, his best friend

Gengenbach was a Catholic village, and the town's schoolhouse was the beautiful old former Catholic monastery that sat just off the main square of Gengenbach. It was an elegant place to go to school, with its beautifully decorated walls and ceilings.

Life was idyllic for Arthur—school, sports, outings, music—with other young girls and boys with whom he had grown up.

Arthur, leaning against the windowsill, is on the right in the third row in this picture

Sitting next to Helmut Breunig in the second row, second from the left, Arthur is holding his beloved mandolin

Chapter Six

Together, he and Helmut played their violins, rode their bikes, and enjoyed hiking in the mountains around their town. The only difference between them was that Arthur attended the town's Hebrew School and became a Bar Mitzvah when he turned thirteen. Helmut was Catholic and attended Mass each Sunday with his family.

In 1903, the Jews of Gengenbach were granted permission to have a Prayer Room in a section of the department store, granted free of charge in a benevolent manner by the Gengenbach municipality. This is where Arthur and the others attended Hebrew School and where Arthur studied for and celebrated his Bar Mitzvah.

The department store in Gengenbach in which the Jews had their Prayer Room

The Jewish families in the town were very close because there were so few of them and because they had lived in the town for generations. Two other Jewish children in Arthur's class in elementary school were Fritz Valfer and Paula Bloch. Another long-time old Gengenbach family, the Blums, had a son named Franz, with whom Arthur was good friends. He also had a very close friendship with Ernst Fetterer, a cousin to the Valfer family. Arthur was very much at home in the Fetterer house.

Chapter Six

Ernst Fetterer and Arthur Meier

Arthur loved music and became so proficient on his violin and mandolin that he was invited to join the Gengenbach String Orchestra. He got great pleasure from playing with the group.

The Gengenbach String Orchestra
Arthur is in the center in the back row

Arthur also loved athletics and joined the Gengenbach Gymnastics Club.

The Gengenbach Gymnastics Club with the instructor, Karl Armbruster Arthur Meier is the first young man at the front of the row and his Jewish classmate Fritz Valfer is standing right behind him

After they graduated from the elementary school in Gengenbach, Arthur and Helmut Breunig began to attend the Oberrealschule Gymnasium in the nearby city of Offenburg. Each morning, the two young men, along with the other boys from Gengenbach who went to the school, would meet at the railroad station across the street from Arthur's house. When the train to Offenburg arrived, the boys would climb into the special car on the train reserved just for them. Late each afternoon, they would finish school and ride the train home. Arthur and Helmut graduated from the Oberrealschule with the class of 1930.

Chapter Six

The class of 1930 from the Oberrealschule in Offenburg. Arthur is standing third from the right in the back row and Helmut is the second from the right in the second row

The Nazis who came to power in 1933 decided that Arthur's charmed life should change.

Chapter Seven

What a Difference a War Makes

1933

> *The beginning of every war is like opening the door into a dark room. One never knows what is hidden in the darkness.*
>
> **Adolf Hitler**

In January of 1933, Reich President Von Hindenburg appointed Adolf Hitler as the Chancellor of Germany, and, by March, an Empowerment Law was passed that cleared the way for Hitler to have power to be the dictator of the country.

Events moved quickly once Hitler was in power. The Treaty of Versailles had caused such German resentment that Hitler was able to capitalize on it rapidly to gain support for his persecution of the Jews, leading eventually to the beginning of the Holocaust, and, finally, to World War II.

Within a month of Hitler's rise to power, there was a boycott of all Jewish shops. On April 11, 1933, the Nazis issued a decree defining a "non-Aryan" as anyone descended from Jewish parents or grandparents, even if he or she had only one parent or grandparent born in the Jewish faith.

The Gestapo was born on April 26, 1933, a creation of Hermann Göring's, a Nazi who was from the German State of Prussia. And finally, many book burnings took place in German towns and cities in 1933.

> *Where they burn books, they also ultimately burn people.*
>
> **Heinrich Heine, "Almansor," 1920**

This quote from Heinrich Heine, a German Jewish poet, was a prophetic foreshadowing of what began to occur in cities all over Germany beginning in March of 1933. There were over 100

Chapter Seven

book burnings in Germany between March and October 1933. The public burnings of books and writings considered un-German were a symbolic prelude to the systematic persecution of the work of Jewish, Marxist, pacifist, and politically undesirable writers considered un-German by the Nazi regime. Jews, liberals, and socialists, especially those socialists connected to the Revolution in Russia, became scapegoats, blamed for undermining the war effort.

These very public displays of "purification" gave the Nazis the opportunity to groom young and impressionable German students. By giving the German youth power and duties for much of what happened in each town, it gave Hitler and Joseph Goebbels, the Propaganda Minister, many opportunities from the earliest days of their rise to power to promote the Aryan culture in the most impressionable young members of the German population. The National Socialist German Students' Association, which had been a stronghold of right-wing radicalism, nationalism, and anti-Semitism since long before 1933, played a central role in this campaign to burn books and other material.

At each book burning, huge numbers of people marched through the streets shouting slogans, singing songs, and gathering at central locations. Surrounded by onlookers, they tossed hundreds of "un-German" books and writings into blazing

A Nazi book burning in 1933 consigned some of Feuchtwanger's work to the flames, along with books by Sigmund Freud and others.

bonfires to bring about the "purification" of Germany.

On the night of May 10, one of the most infamous of the book burnings occurred on Munich's Königsplatz, led by students from local universities, members of the Hitler Youth, the SA and SS groups, and the "Kampfbund für deutsche Kultur," the "Combat League for German Culture." The book burnings of May 10 were the culmination of the "Aktion wider den undeutschen Geist," the "Campaign against the un-German" Spirit." This was an important and highly symbolic stage for the National Socialist German Workers Party, the official name of the Nazi Party, in their bid to establish power on the local level and among young Germans.

In Baden, many book burnings took place around June 20, the Summer Solstice, a traditional time in Germany for bonfires. One such event took place in the state capital of Karlsruhe on Saturday, June 17, at which a famous son of Offenburg, Otto Wacker, now the Minister of Culture and Education, spoke in person.

The book burning which took place in Offenburg was appalling. The population was asked to participate: "Every self-respecting German is called upon to hand over Jewish scandal and dirt books to the responsible Hitler Youth leadership. The Hitler Youth will go through the streets to collect the Jewish trash and filthy literature and hand it over to the fire on Saturday evening. The Offenburger who is still in possession of such a filthy book after the collection is not a decent real German." At the fire, which included many students and teachers, the participants chanted:

<u>Flamme Empori</u>

    Flame up, rise with blazing light from the mountains to the Rhine, glowing up.
    See we stand, faithful in the consecrated circle, to see thee to the fatherland's praise, flame.
    On all heights, shine thou flaming sign, that all enemies pale when they see thee.
    Holy glow. Call the youth together, that by the blazing flames, courage grows.

Chapter Seven

Shining glow, see how singing couples swear at the altar of flame to be Germans.
Hear the word Father on life and death, help us acquire freedom, be our refuge.

The chant was followed by several magical ritual sayings, all ending with "Un-German spirit burn!"

Arthur Meier had graduated only three years earlier from the Oberrealschule in Offenburg—it is very likely some of his classmates and teachers were among those taking part in throwing books and materials into the blazing fire, singing "Flamme Empori," and shouting "un-German spirit burn!" How horrifying and frightening that must have been for him.

And finally, it seems that book burning also actually took place in Gengenbach on June 17, 1933! The story of what took place was described in a newspaper article which was printed in the Gengenbach Weekly of "The Kinzig Messenger" on June 20, 1933. Gengenbach is a small village. The chances are very high that Arthur Meier witnessed what went on in the Market Square, not far from his house. It is hard to imagine the sense of betrayal, helplessness, and lack of control over his destiny that this would have caused him. Is it perhaps possible that some of the material burned "from individual families" came from the Meier house on Grünstraße?

> **Gengenbach,** den 20. Juni 1933.
> [Zur Bekämpfung von Schmutz und Schund] wurde von der hiesigen Hitlerjugend vergangene Woche eine Sammlung der entsprechenden Literatur bei den einzelnen Familien veranstaltet. Am Samstag abend wurde das gesammelte Material sowie Fahnen der marxistischen Partei auf dem Marktplatze feierlich verbrannt.

The Kinzig Messenger, Gengenbach, the 20, June 1933

To combat dirt and filth, the local Hitler Youth organized a collection of relevant material from the individual families last week. On Saturday evening, June 17, 1933, the collected material and flags of the Marxist party were solemnly burned on the Market Square.

Reading the translation of that article, while knowing what evil was to follow in the years to come in Germany, answers the question of why applying for a visa to leave Germany as quickly as possible became imperative for Arthur Meier.

The closing of the community's synagogue in 1934 was the next public affront to the Jewish Community of Gengenbach. In 1934, the community of 30 Jews were evicted from their Prayer Room because they were now to be charged an unaffordable sum of 30 Reichsmarks for its use.

The days of benevolence toward Gengenbach's Jews were over. Now it was time for all Jews who could get out of Gengenbach to leave their once-beautiful little village.

On September 15, 1935, the Nuremberg Racial Laws were put into effect. They excluded Jews completely from German society.

Chapter Eight

Leaving a Charmed Life

August 1937

The sequence of Nazi atrocities in Germany beginning in 1933, often led by his neighbors and school friends in Gengenbach and Offenburg, led Arthur Meier to apply for a visa in 1933. On May 19, 1937, after four years of petitioning the United States for permission to enter, Arthur Meier finally got a visa from the U.S. government that allowed him to get a passport and book passage on a ship to America. History would show that the American Consulate in Stuttgart was the most difficult consulate in all of Europe from which to get a visa.

The changes in Germany between the time he was born in July 1910 and August 1937 made 27-year-old Arthur Meier put his steamer trunk on the train at the station in Gengenbach, hug his weeping parents for the last time, and climb on the train to Offenburg, where he would change to a train for Strasbourg, then one to Paris, and ultimately, to a ship going to America.

Chapter Eight

In front of the beautiful carved doorway of 27 Grünstraße are five of the six Meier children born in the house. From left to right, standing in the back are Berthold Meier, his wife Sophie Roland Meier, the only one not born in the house in Gengenbach, and his son Arthur Meier. Seated on the top step are Sophie Meier Wiegel (left) and Rosa Meier Libkind (right) and the little lady on the bottom step is Elise Meier Daube. Sadly, this picture was the last time the Meier children, minus their baby brother Emil who was in Reading, Pennsylvania, were together.

By 1954, four of the six people in the picture would be dead. Berthold Meier, Sophie Roland Meier and Elise Meier Daube would all end up together at Camp de Gurs in France. Sophie Roland Meier would be the first to die, from starvation, at Gurs on January 13, 1942. Elise would end up transported to Auschwitz where she would die in 1942 and Berthold to Maidanek/Sobibor where he would suffer the same fate in 1943. Arthur would get out of Germany but would live only until 1954, suffering from a heart condition that would kill him at the age of 43, when he would die of a massive coronary. Rosa and Sophie both would live out the war—Rosa running throughout the war in France from the Nazis after their occupation of Paris, and Sophie in Gernrode, Germany, safely married to a non-Jewish husband. The Nazis would be very successful in their effort to get rid of the Meier family.

The story of this photograph sadly illustrates the reasons for Arthur Meier's departure from his parents, his friends, his home, and the life he loved in his beloved Germany—the Germany that had been a charmed homeland to his family for such a very long time.

Arthur celebrated his 27th birthday on July 24, 1937 with his dear parents, and soon left for Paris where he stayed with his Aunt Rosa, his father's sister. His postcard to his Uncle Emil, their younger brother in Reading, sent from Paris, is the only example we have in Arthur's own words what he was feeling about leaving Germany.

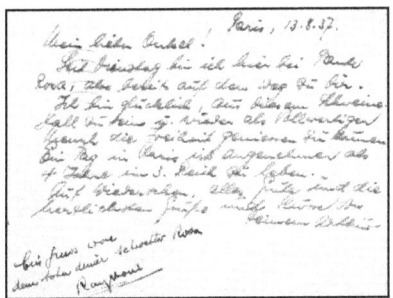 

Paris, 13.8.37

My Dear Uncle!

I've been here with Aunt Rosa in Paris since Tuesday, so I'm already on my way to you. I am happy to be out of this pigsty and to be able to enjoy freedom again as a full-fledged human being. A day in Paris is more pleasant than living in the Third Reich for four years.

Goodbye, all the best and the warmest greetings and kisses from
Your, Arthur

Chapter Eight

Arthur Meier sailed from LeHavre, France and landed in New York on Friday, August 27, 1937 aboard the S.S. President Roosevelt. He headed for Reading, Pennsylvania to join his Uncle Emil, having no idea that he would never see his beautiful town of Gengenbach again. He also did not know that he would never again see his beloved parents, Berthold and Sophie Meier, who would both die in remarkably terrible ways, as would many of his family members and his friends. He would never see his friend, Helmut Breunig, again.

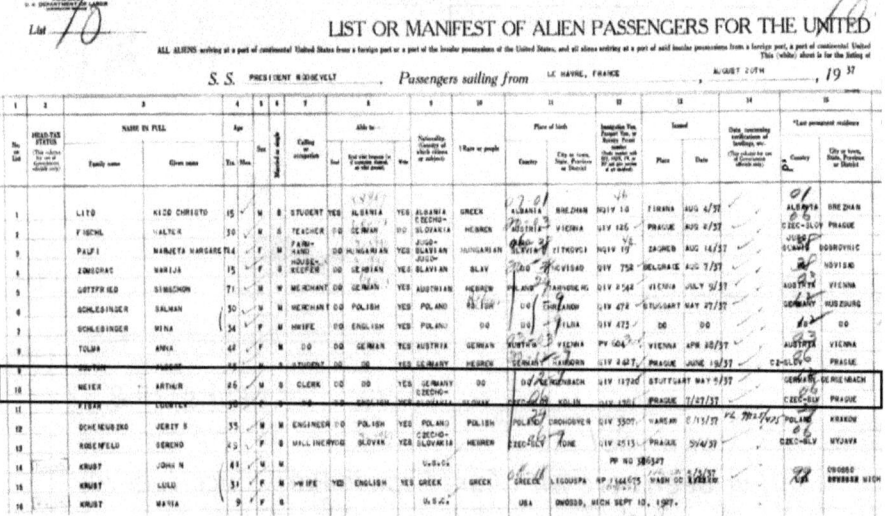

Arthur Meier's charmed existence was over.

Looking back more than eighty years, we know what lay in front of him when he wrote the postcard from Paris. How fortunate that he did not know.

Chapter Nine

A Surprise on the Internet

Within days of arriving home in Miami, I looked up the *Stolpersteine* project on the Internet. I found out that Gunter Demnig, a German whose father had been a Nazi, had started the project in 2000. His email address, along with dozens of other contact peoples' towns and email addresses filled pages on his website. I searched, but Gengenbach, the town my father came from, was not on the list of contacts. I hadn't expected it to be—it is really only a village, but I did see a name of a contact from Offenburg, the nearby small city where my father had gone to high school. I composed an email to Demnig, and, at the last minute, I added the email address of the woman from Offenburg, Gerda-Marie Lüttgen, to his.

Days went by as I waited to hear from Demnig. But to my surprise, it was Gerda-Marie, the woman from Offenburg, to whom I had impulsively also sent the email at the last minute, who answered me on June 5th. Her email contained only a link:

https://www.bo.de/lokales/kinzigtal/
namen-der-opfer-sind-zurueckgekehrt

I clicked on the link and found myself looking at a page from a newspaper from Offenburg, written in German, which I can't read, with a photograph of a group of people standing in the rain in the center of the page. As I stared at the picture, it changed—to another one of more people standing around with umbrellas. Then it changed again, and I found myself staring in confusion at a photograph of *Stolpersteine* with my grandparents' names on them. I wondered if I was hallucinating—had I made their *Stolpersteine* appear just by wishing that I could? The picture changed again, twice—the last two views were also of *Stolpersteine* of members of the Valfer family, one of the other Jewish families who lived in Gengenbach. I must have spent

Chapter Nine

fifteen minutes watching the pictures change, over and over, until I had seen my grandparents' names often enough to believe that I hadn't conjured up this vision. Their *Stolpersteine* were real!

The Stolpersteine with my grandparents' names on them

The 2009 newspaper article telling about the installation by Gunter Demnig of six Stolpersteine in Gengenbach in memory of six of the town's Jews who died in the Holocaust

Completely overwhelmed, and desperate to translate the newspaper page, I called my son Adam and told him the story. "Copy the words into Google Translate, Mom," he said. "It will translate them for you."

I did what Adam said—and discovered that what it said in the newspaper article was utterly astounding. Now I understood that Gunter Demnig had installed the *Stolpersteine* in front of my grandparents' house in 2009. The project to get them done had been carried out by teachers and students of the Marta-Schanzenbach-Gymnasium in Gengenbach.

The article went on to explain that the inspiration for the teachers and students had been a book called *700 Years of Jewish Life in Gengenbach 1308—2008* by Dr. Martin Ruch. What the students read in the book about the history of the Jews of their own town in the years beginning in 1933 had horrified them. To attempt to memorialize the tragedy that happened to their own Jewish townspeople, especially some of those who had died in the Holocaust, they began the project of putting *Stolpersteine* in front of the houses in Gengenbach where these six dead Jews had lived.

And, so, I discovered, my grandparents' markers had already been done—in 2009—thanks to some very special teachers and students. Thanks also to Dr. Ruch, a historian from nearby Offenburg, whose research and book gave birth to the project.

What I read and saw made me wish I had been there, standing in the rain, watching the dedication of my grandparents' *Stolpersteine*. I quickly emailed back to Gerda-Marie.

And then I wrote to the city officials of Gengenbach. I desperately needed to find Martin Ruch!

Chapter Ten

Serendipity

Serendipity is the only way to explain how my whole world changed on July 16, 2017, when I got an email from Dr. Martin Ruch. There is no better way to explain finding my angel from Offenburg and the years of serendipity that followed.

> *July 16, 2017*
>
> *Dear Mrs. Katz,*
>
> *I got your mail from Mr. Goetz, City Administration, and would like to answer your question. I wrote a book about the Jewish community of Gengenbach (including two pictures of your grandparents) and also some books about the Jews in Offenburg (where I was born 1950). Actually, I collect for a biography about Eva Mendelsson, born 1931 in Gengenbach but living in Offenburg. Sent in 1940 with mother and sister to Gurs. Ended up in 1944 in Switzerland. Today in England. That's about me. You collect for a Meier family history?*
> **If I can help, please ask,**
> *Martin*
>
> ---
>
> *Kulturagentur*
> *Dr. Martin Ruch*
> *Waldseestraße 53*
> *77731 Willstätt*

If I can help, please ask...

Help?! I'd been looking for help for seventeen years since I returned from my trip to Gurs. Since 2000, when I decided it was time to give up the carefully constructed mental cave in which the Holocaust and I lived, I hadn't been able to find anyone to help me do it.

Chapter Ten

You bet you can help!

I was elated to get a response from Martin Ruch. I answered him immediately. Perhaps here was the person who could translate the letters for me?

The letters...

I sat in my office, staring at the familiar stack of my father's mail in my closet—postcards and letters—that had been sitting around my whole life, thanks to my mother, Sylvia Wise Meier, whose love for my father had made her schlep around and preserve so many of the things he brought from Germany—the trunk, the violin and mandolin, the monogrammed linens, the silver pieces, the ring, the green photo album, and most importantly, the pile of letters written to my father from Gurs and from relatives and friends in the years that followed his departure. Those letters, all written in German, could hold the secrets that would make it possible for me to find my grandparents and tell their story.

If Martin Ruch was going to translate my letters for me, the question was...how was I going to get these fragile, elderly documents into his hands? Luckily, we live in the 21st century and we have computers, printers, and...scanners! I called Adam. *When can you help me scan my father's letters now that I have somebody to translate them?*

The envelopes had not been opened in 75 years. I had never in my life bothered to even open them because I knew I couldn't read what was in them. I had no idea in what condition they would be. I also had never put them in any order. That alone would be a big job—the postmarks were often hard to read and so each letter had to be pried out of the envelope carefully to see the date it was written. I had never really paid attention to who the writer was, and, now I had to figure that out so I could arrange them by date and by author. Some of the writers were names I had never heard before. And, of course, there was nobody to ask...

Adam and I spent hours opening each letter gingerly, placing the envelopes and the letters on the scanner carefully and then organizing each set of scans with a date.

A memorable thing happened when Adam took out one letter. Out fell a heart! A heart? Yes, a hand-made paper heart! Luckily, the note on the front of the heart was written in French, which I know, so I could read it.

The Students of Camp de Gurs

**We have the honor of sending you
our best wishes for Mother's Day**

Gurs May 1941

Chapter Ten

This was the first time I had ever seen the heart, because the letter out of which it came was one of those that I had never ever opened. What shocked Adam and me the most, I think, was the sudden realization that there were children at Gurs. Knowing how dreadful the conditions in the camp were—the starvation, the filth, the winter cold and summer heat, the constant rain, the crowded conditions—which the children were living through—horrified us.

And yet, someone had encouraged the children to make hearts and write Mother's Day cards to the women of the camp. Such a positive thing to do for children living in the middle of hell. Both Adam and I, teachers that we were, understood what an astounding gift this had been to the children who made the cards, as well as to the women who received them.

Later, when Martin translated the letter from my grandfather out of which the heart fell, we discovered that his writing did not refer to the heart at all. I assume that he included the Mother's Day card in his letter to my father to show him what his mother had gotten. The letter itself spoke mostly about food—and how everyone at Gurs was starving. The letters were all filled with begging—for food, for money, for warm clothes. How shocking and difficult it would have been for people who had lived perfectly normal, middle-class lives in the towns in Baden up until October 22, 1940. How helpless my father must have felt when he read the letters.

When Adam and I finished scanning the letters from Gurs, I had to keep myself from sending them all to Martin at one time. I restrained myself and sent him the first letter.

Chapter Eleven

The Month from Hell

November 1938

My father arrived in America in August 1937, his visa guaranteed by his father's younger brother, Emil Meier. Why Emil Meier had ended up in Reading, Pennsylvania by 1917, as shown by his draft registration, is and will probably remain, a complete mystery. Ironically, if he had become an American soldier, Emil and his brother, Berthold, would have ended up fighting on opposing sides in World War I.

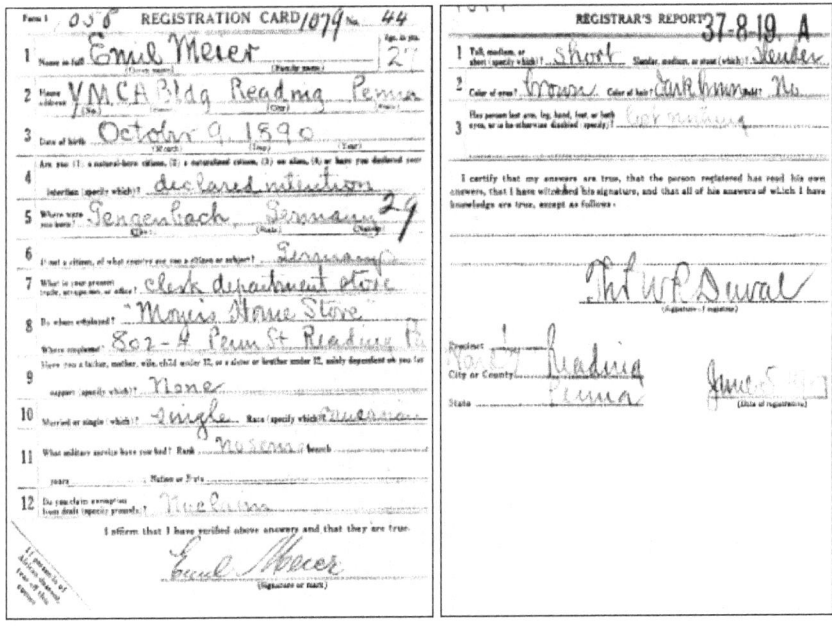

Emil Meier's 1917 draft registration in Reading

When Arthur Meier got to Reading in 1937, he probably knew only his Uncle Emil and Herman Bodenheimer, the man he had met at the American Embassy in Stuttgart. My father's first job when he came to Reading was working for Max Fisher at Tru-Tex Hosiery Mills, in Mohnton, a neighboring town, which must have been the one that guaranteed my father the right to get a

Chapter Eleven

visa and a passport to come to the U.S. His Uncle Emil worked in a men's clothing store in Reading, so how he or my father were connected with Max Fisher in Reading's hosiery industry remains another mystery lost to the ages.

Arthur and his Uncle Emil, his father's brother, in Reading, PA

```
                 Front
Meichel Mary (wid Lawrence) r135 N
    Front
Meier Arth slsmn r328 N 2d
 "  Emil clk Joseph's Economy Stores r
    328 N 2d
 "  Helen D student r1015 Bellevue av
    (Laureldale)
 "  John (Sarah F) eng Met Edison Co
    h Fleetwood
 "  Jos M (Ruth A) adv agt h1015 Bellevue
```

Arthur and Emil Meier's entries in the 1938 Reading phone book for the apartment they shared on 2nd Street

Reading, PA was once known as "The Nation's Full-Fashioned Hosiery Center." How extremely ironic that my father ended up in <u>this business </u>in <u>this place</u> after fleeing from Nazi Germany! A suburb of Reading, named Wyomissing, was the home of three German men who made their fortunes at Berkshire Knitting Mills and its textile affiliates, in a business they had learned in Germany. Ferdinand Thun, Henry Janssen, and Gustav Oberlaender were also major financial supporters of the German American Bund, an infamous group of Nazi-loving Germans in the United States. At the Wyomissing Fire Company's Banquet Hall there were swastikas painted on the outside of the walls of the building! These notorious Nazi-loving men were also thought to have been major contributors to the building of the Nazi Stadium in Nuremberg, Germany, from where many of Hitler's famous speeches were delivered. It is very interesting and puzzling that several Jewish men also became very successful in the hosiery business in Reading, including, apparently Max Fisher.

One year after my father got to Reading, the news reached America about what had just gone on in Germany on November 9th and 10th, 1938, with tragic stories and pictures of "Kristallnacht" and what was happening afterward. How my father must have felt hearing all of this is quite hard to fathom. I do not know when he learned that his father and friends had been among those arrested and sent to Dachau. With his mother now alone in Gengenbach, the pain he must have felt is unimaginable. And the helplessness he must have felt at his inability to do anything for his beloved parents is incredibly sad.

I suspect that what I am about to tell you next, dear reader, is going to be almost impossible for you to believe. I wish it were a figment of my imagination, but it's not. One week after Kristallnacht, on November 17, 1938, Emil Meier, Arthur's uncle, committed suicide—and not because of what was happening to his family in Germany! All I know about the circumstances surrounding Emil's suicide is one fact my mother told me. Apparently, Emil had a relationship with a married woman who refused to divorce her husband. In despair, Emil jumped out of a window of the Abraham Lincoln Hotel on Fifth Street in

Chapter Eleven

downtown Reading, the fall killing him instantly. According to his death certificate, he was only 48 years old. That's it—that's all I know—his suicide had nothing to do with Kristallnacht, but was, rather, for unrequited love.

Where and when my father learned of his uncle's unfortunate death I have no idea, nor do I know if it came as a surprise to him that his uncle was so despondent as to commit suicide in such a dreadful way. It was never discussed in my family.

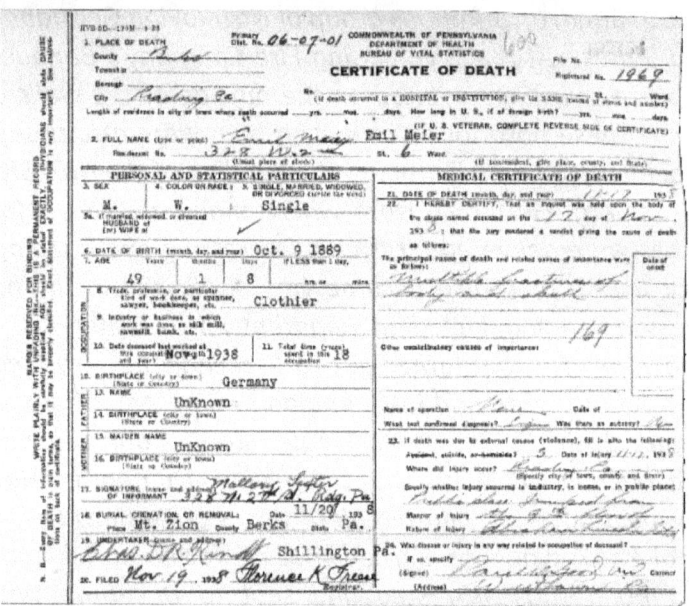

Emil Meier's Death Certificate

Two of the Jewish synagogues in Reading—the Orthodox and the Conservative—did not allow the bodies of people who committed suicide to be buried in their cemeteries. The Reform Temple, somewhat more modern, allowed my father to have his uncle buried <u>outside</u> the actual fence of its cemetery.

Years later, when Alan Weitzman was the Rabbi of that Temple, he found and gave me the receipt for Emil Meier's gravesite. The grave cost $100 in 1938, but it does not say who paid for it. I assume it was my father.

How my father dealt with this tragedy is beyond my comprehension. All of this while listening to the news coming *from Germany about Kristallnacht, including the news that his father was now imprisoned at Dachau! How I wish I had asked my mother more questions about this time. The only positive thing about the Emil Meier story is that at least he lived long enough to help my father get safely to America.*

The Abraham Lincoln Hotel opened on March 23, 1930 as a large and very grand hotel in downtown Reading. A room rented for $2.99 a night! The hotel is famous for two events which occurred there: Eleanor Roosevelt spoke from a balcony in the hotel lobby and John Phillip Sousa, the famous composer of marches such as "Stars and Stripes Forever," suffered a heart attack and died at the hotel after conducting Reading's Ringgold Band on March 6, 1932. Six years after Sousa died of natural causes, Emil Meier also died at the Abraham Lincoln Hotel in 1938, but, heaven knows, <u>not</u> of natural causes!

I lived in Reading from the time I was eleven years old until I got married in 1965. The Abraham Lincoln Hotel, with its large ballroom and smaller party rooms was often the scene of parties, dances, and later, weddings that I was invited to. Although I always went, it felt uncomfortable for me to be there. When I got invitations that said, "Abraham Lincoln Hotel," I always shuddered. But I certainly never was comfortable telling anyone that I hated the Abraham Lincoln Hotel and certainly not why I hated it.

Chapter Twelve

Kristallnacht: Night of Broken Glass

November 9-10, 1938

Adolf Hitler came to power in 1933, and immediately began to persecute the German Jews, whom he blamed for Germany's defeat in World War I, along with the many other crimes which he held against them. Hitler's goal during the first part of the Holocaust was to rid Germany of all its Jews by getting them to move to other parts of the world. However, getting the rest of the world to accept them as immigrants was entirely another matter for the Jews of Germany and the rest of Europe. As you already read, it took my father, Arthur Meier, four years to get a visa to immigrate to the United States.

By 1937, life had become a shocking hell for the Jews living in Germany. Much to Hitler's dismay, however, the Jewish population in Germany in 1937 had fallen only 35%, even though their lives and businesses had all come to a standstill.

The Nazis quickly learned that they could get away with a great deal of abuse against the Jews without much resistance from either the German residents or the outside world. Therefore, even incidents like the one in Nußbach in 1938, revolting as it was, didn't accomplish what Hitler wanted. A few months before Kristallnacht in 1938, a group of townspeople in Nußbach, Germany met in the courtyard of the "Zur Linde Inn." They are shown in this photo having great fun, ridiculing the Jews of the town by staging a parody of them, parading through the village streets with a sign that says, "To Jerusalem." The villagers are dressed in black, with large noses, wearing tall hats, and carrying sacks and bags. At the end of the parade in the Town Hall Square, the "Jews" are shown to be auctioning off their goat and other belongings.

Chapter Twelve

The Nazis had to do something quickly to change the small number of Jews leaving Germany! An opportunity for what Hitler wanted landed in his lap on November 7, 1938. Herschel Grynszpan, a German Jewish refugee living illegally with relatives in Paris, walked into the German Embassy in Paris, shooting and killing a diplomat, the third secretary, Ernst vom Rath.

Finally, Adolf Hitler had the excuse he had been looking for to speed up the pace of his plan to rid Germany of every last Jew. Two days later, on November 9th, Hitler declared an assault against the Jews, claiming self-defense for vom Rath's death. He opened the floodgates of destruction and violence against the Jews of Germany—an event now known as **Kristallnacht—The Night of Broken Glass.**

If you ask most people what they imagine when they hear the word "Kristallnacht," they would describe the burning of synagogues and the broken store front windows in Berlin and other German cities.

The Meier family did not live in Berlin. They lived in the

tiny village of Gengenbach in the Ortenau Region of the state of Baden, close to the Rhine River, which served as the border between France and Germany. So, what did Kristallnacht look like in Offenburg, the nearby city, and in Gengenbach itself? What was the effect of "The Night of Broken Glass" on Sophie and Berthold Meier and the other Jews of their small village in the Black Forest?

On November 9th in Offenburg, SS flags were flying everywhere. A speech given by Hitler from Munich was broadcast over loudspeakers in the city. SS applicants were sworn in at the front of the SS district office. Next, the district leader Karl Rombach spoke. Afterward, the SA and SS men went to pubs to celebrate their promotions. Later, a telex from the Chief of the State Security Police, Heydrich, arrived with instructions to "arrest as many Jews in the district—especially wealthy ones—as can be accommodated in the existing prisons."

On the evening of November 9th, in Gengenbach, there was a commemoration in the Monastery Square in memory of vom Rath "who had just died in Paris for his fatherland by Jewish assassination." Fortunately, the event ended without a huge outburst of rage against the Jews of Gengenbach, with only small incidents such as the smashing of the Valfer and Fetterer's textile shop windows on the Market Square.

Early the next morning of November 10th, in Offenburg, a group of National Socialist men destroyed the interior of the Synagogue (Salmen). At 5 PM, a "rally" in Offenburg began in front of the Hotel Palmengarten, during which the Jewish Café Weil and the synagogue were devastated by SS and SD guards and a crowd of local citizens. The riots ended by 8 PM with the burning of objects from the synagogue in front of the town hall, after which some National Socialists went to a concert of the local orchestra scheduled for the evening.

Gengenbach was, of course, in the Offenburg district. Early on the morning of November 10th, the police showed up at the Meier house, as well as at the households of all of the Jewish men of Gengenbach. According to an article in the "Kinzigboten," the local newspaper, an order for anti-Jewish actions was issued from

Chapter Twelve

Munich and from Berlin, "In order to prevent riots against the Jews, which were to be expected in justified indignation after the news of the death of the legation councilor vom Rath who had fallen for Germany, all adult male Jews in the districts of Kehl, Lahr, Offenburg, and Wolfach were to be taken into protective custody on Wednesday at dawn."

The arrests were probably not noticed by the Jews' neighbors because they were done early in the morning and without much fanfare. Few Germans even knew that in all about 36,000 German Jewish men were sent by bus or train to the Concentration Camps of Buchenwald, Dachau, and Sachsenhausen.

The men from Gengenbach, including my grandfather, were placed in police squad cars and driven to Offenburg, where they were placed in the city's prison. Awaiting their arrival at the Offenburg railway station were the trains ready to take them to Dachau. A rope was stretched around the entire train "so nothing would happen to the Jews."

The number of Jews arrested in Offenburg and the surrounding towns and sent to the prison began to grow as the day wore on. An SS man named Schwab came to the prison repeatedly during the day to hold singing rehearsals with the prisoners, practicing various modified verses of the German folk song, "Muss I denn Zum Städtele Hinaus: Must I, must I leave the town, When I come, When I never come again."

SS-Sturmbannführer Brand also came to the prison several times during the day, and on his orders, another SS leader, Volk, put cylinder-shaped hats on the heads of many of the Jews. Brand also made one of the prisoners read to the others from Hitler's "<u>Mein Kampf</u>."

The march of about 80 Jewish men to the train in Offenburg that evening was completely shameful. It began about 9 PM and took over an hour, although only a short distance, through the center of Offenburg. On the way, the Jewish men had to sing "Muss I denn" while being insulted, kicked, and beaten by bystanders and SS men, some using the butts of their rifles. The SS leader, Volk, kicked a lawyer named Schleicher. At Brand's orders, Schwab was careful to see that every prisoner sang along, *yelling at the Jews he thought were not singing loud enough, shouting "Sing louder you pigs!"*

The German folksong, "Muss I denn zum Städtele hinaus" "Must I leave the town" is a famous and popular highly sentimental folk song. The words were added to a traditional melody and published by Friedrich Silcher in 1827, and quickly made popular as a soldier and traveler's song. The song was abused by the Nazis as part of the mockery of the Jews and opponents of the regime and was sung at the deportation of Jews in many cities in Germany. It is an extremely popular and well-known folk song that is sung to this day. Several pop singers have interpreted it in their own individual ways, including Elvis Presley whose song "Wooden Heart" was based on the German folksong.

Chapter Twelve

At 11 PM the train left the station from Offenburg, but the men on the train had no idea they were headed for Dachau until well into the trip. They were not given anything to eat during the three-day journey.

Dachau was the first Concentration Camp built by the Nazis in Germany. It was used from March 1933, to April 1945, when it was liberated by the U.S. Army. It was operated by the SS and used originally to house political prisoners: Communists, Romani (Gypsies), homosexuals, Jehovah's Witnesses, and Catholic priests. After Kristallnacht, over 10,000 of the German Jewish men who had been arrested on the morning of November 10, 1938 were sent there. Most were released after a month or two when they agreed to emigrate from Germany, but some men died during their stay at the camp.

November 10, 1938, is depicted in these photographs from a famous town in the Black Forest, Baden Baden, near Gengenbach. These Jewish men were sent to the Dachau Camp.

In Baden Baden, the Jews are forced to march with "God does not forgive us" signs after Kristallnacht

Kristallnacht: Night of Broken Glass

When Berthold Meier was sent to Dachau on November 10, 1938, ironically, it had been less than twenty years since he had been liberated from the French prisoner of war camp as a German soldier. In less than twenty years, he went from being a German soldier imprisoned by the French, to being a Jew imprisoned by the same Germans for whom he had fought. His stay at Dachau was recorded in Book No. 104/22467 as having lasted from November 11, 1938 to December 15, 1938 when he was sent back home to Gengenbach.

The release of the eight men from Gengenbach who had been deported to Dachau is recorded in the Gestapo's "Judenkartei (Jewish File)." On December 9, 1938, a letter was sent to the district offices: "I request that the Jews arrested on the occasion of the action against Jewry on November 10, 1938 and transferred to the Dachau Concentration Camp be reported immediately and continuously to the Karlsruhe State Police Headquarters after the return to their place of residence, stating their name, first, date and place of birth."

*Following directions, on December 20, 1938, the Gengenbach police reported: "…**that the Jews Adolf Valfer, Isaak Valfer, Louis Valfer, Sigmund Bloch, and Berthold Meier, who lived here had returned from Dachau.**" These five men were the older generation among the Jews of the town. Berthold Meier* *and the others were allowed to leave Dachau on the promise that they would leave Germany, their families' homeland for hundreds of years, the homeland Berthold fought for in World War I. All German Jews had to promise to give up all their valuable possessions, to surrender everything they owned, from the Rothschilds in Frankfurt on down to Berthold Meier in Gengenbach.*

*Added on January 7, 1939 was: **"The subsequently listed Jews have returned here today from Dachau—Ernst Fetterer, b. 1906, Jakob Valfer, b. 1906, and Fritz Valfer, b. 1910."** These three younger men were my father's friends. Fritz Valfer, who was born the same year as my father, was in his class in school in Gengenbach.*

The only name missing from the list of the younger generation of Jewish men in Gengenbach was that of Arthur Meier, who on January 7, 1939 was living safely in Reading, Pennsylvania.

According to Dr. Martin Ruch, "From now on, the path led to the Holocaust. The persecution and extermination had no longer been publicly conceived and implemented on the streets, but quietly by administrative officials and the SS."

Chapter Thirteen

Baking Lebkuchen

February 1939

The orders are very clear—the Jews of Germany are to turn in all their valuable jewelry, art, silver and gold, furs, and warm coats—to the German police by the end of March. This is to pay for all of the damage caused on Kristallnacht, the night of the trouble in November. The Jews were the ones terrorized and abused, and yet they are the ones being forced to pay for the damage—a one billion Reichsmark collective fine and all of their valuable possessions.

Since Berthold got back from the Dachau Concentration Camp, he is very frail. He wanders around the house like a lost soul. Sophie Meier understands her husband's shock—he thinks of himself as German first, then as a Jew. He spent five years in the prison camp in France as a German soldier in the last war. Now he is only a Jew to the Germans. Less than human...told to leave the country his family has lived in for hundreds of years.

As she thinks about what she has to give up, Sophie's eyes fall on her hand, at the gold and diamond ring that her mother, Jette Roland, always wore and that she gave Sophie the day her daughter married Berthold Meier. Sophie never takes it off. She tried to get her son Arthur to take it when he left for America, but he refused—he said it was too special to her for him to take it. Arthur—not the Nazis—must have the ring!

Sophie Meier walks to the pantry and begins to collect the ingredients for making lebkuchen.

Chapter Fourteen

What They Did Not Get

June 1939

Arthur and Sylvia Meier come home from work to find a note from their mailman that he tried to deliver a box but could not because they were at work. It is a long night of waiting and trying to imagine whom the box is from and what is in it.

The next morning, Arthur stops at the Post Office on 5th Street on his way to work. It shocks him when the clerk brings out a tattered cardboard box.

"Wow, Mr. Meier," the mailman says to him, "This box was mailed in March—it took four months to get here from Germany!"

After Arthur signs for the box, he goes to work. At least now he knows who sent the box—the handwriting is his mother's. He decides to wait and open the box when he gets home—to do it with Sylvia. All day long he looks at the box sitting on his desk, wondering what his mother might have sent him.

He takes the box home after work. As he opens the door to his apartment, he sees Sylvia in the kitchen, making their dinner. She walks over and looks at what he is carrying.

"Arthur! It's from your mother!" Sylvia says with surprise. "What is it?" She covers the kitchen table with an old towel and then he puts the box down.

"I have no idea, but it took four months to get here," he says. By this time, Sylvia is standing next to him, eyeing the box, which is tied shut by a piece of string, the string knotted so tightly that she goes to the drawer, takes out scissors, and hands them to him. When the string finally comes off, Arthur begins carefully peeling off the tattered paper covering the cardboard box. Finally, he impatiently lifts off the lid of the box.

Inside, wrapped in brown paper, is something round and deep and metal. As soon as he sees the red flowers, he realizes that he is looking at his mother's favorite biscuit tin. When he was a boy, she would scold him if she caught him stealing cookies from it just before dinner. "You'll spoil your appetite!" she would always

Chapter Fourteen

say. He feels a huge wave of sadness come over him as he gazes down on something that is so special to his mother.

"Don't tell me she sent me cookies!" he says, laughing with tears rolling down his cheeks.

Another piece of string holds the tin closed, and tucked inside the string is a note in his mother's beautiful handwriting. He translates the German into English for Sylvia. His mother writes that she hopes they are both well and enjoying married life. Then she writes, "My Dearest Arthur, I have baked your favorite lebkuchen. Eat all of them yourself!"

Arthur turns and looks at his wife with a puzzled look on his face. "My mother would never say that to me. She spent my whole life trying to get me to share with others. She worried that I would be a spoiled only child just like she was. What is in this biscuit tin?"

He cuts the string, lifts off the lid, and there, wrapped in white paper are...lebkuchen, his favorite cookies! Hard as rocks, but nevertheless, lebkuchen. He and Sylvia look at each other.

"Your mother is so sensible. Why would she send you cookies she knew would be rocks by the time you got them?" Sylvia asks.

"I agree," Arthur says, nodding his head. "Maybe they are not just cookies. We need to soak these cookies in a basin of water."

Without another word, Sylvia walks over to the kitchen sink and gets the dishpan out from the cabinet underneath it. She fills the pan with water and brings it over to the kitchen table and puts it next to the biscuit tin and all the wrapping. Lovingly, Arthur takes each cookie from the tin and gently puts it in the water.

When he goes to bed that night, the cookies are still sitting in the water, exactly as he left them. When Arthur wakes up in the morning, he heads directly for the kitchen. Sylvia is already there, ahead of him, waiting. She takes him by the hand, leads him to the kitchen table, and points to the pan.

There, lying among the now-crumbled lebkuchen, he sees something gold. He reaches down, dips his hand into the water, and lifts out his mother's gold and diamond ring. As Sylvia opens her arms, he moves into them, putting his head down on her shoulder. Between sobs he says, "It was my grandmother Jette's ring. She gave it to my mother when my parents got married. My mother never took it off."

*FOR THE RECORD: WHAT THEY DID GET

Abschrift								
Annahme Nr. 187 Tag: 29.3.1939		Ablieferer: Meier Berthold, Gengenbach, Grünstr. 13						
Eingang	Ge- wicht	Gold	Schmuck	Münzen	Kunst- sachen	Silber	Altsilber	zusammen
2 Tafellöffel	115						2,30	
1 Salatbesteck	20					0,40		
Bruchsilber	3						0,06	
1 Herrenuhrgehäuse	22	35,20						
1 Damenuhrgehäuse	4,8	9,60						
Bruchgold 14 kt.y	61	97,60						
Bruchgold 14 kt.	8	12,80						
2 Plomben 18 kt.	3	6,-						
		161,20	-	-	-	0,40	2,36	163,96

This is a photocopy of the document which lists the valuables* Berthold Meier turned into the police station in Gengenbach on March 29, 1939. Notice that there is no gold and diamond ring on the list. On the day Sophie and Berthold were required to hand in their valuables, the ring was on its way to Arthur Meier in Reading, Pennsylvania, nestled safely in a lebkuchen.

Chapter Fifteen

Starting A New Life

It appears that my parents met shortly after my father got to Reading. I have no idea who introduced them nor when they formed a relationship.

Even though they were living in the same city when they were dating, my parents wrote letters to each other frequently. Thank heavens for the fact that this was the 1930's, and while telephones had achieved fairly widespread use by then, a family's telephone sat on a phone bench, consisting of a seat and a connected table. The phone did not move because it was wired to the wall. Personal calls were difficult because many people, including the Wise family, had what was called a "party line," which they shared with another family.

Therefore, one of the gifts the gods gave me is that my mother saved the box of letters from my father to her, and my brother gave them to me after she died in 2012. Sadly, I had never really paid attention to their existence, nor had I read them earlier, and, so, I never asked her about them. Looking back now at the letters my father wrote my mother during that time, I realize that there were a million questions I wish I had asked her. I didn't, and so, I have a lot of never-to-be-answered questions.

After he met my mother, my father must have been thrilled to discover that he had more or less walked into what he had left behind in Germany. There was a large group of young Jewish men and women his age. The women, including my mother, belonged to "The Deborah Club," a collection of eligible, attractive young women. There seemed to be an equal number of eligible, handsome young men to match. After my parents became a couple, they are clearly enjoying themselves together in this picture from a Deborah Club event in 1939.

The photos and letters from my parents' courtship and early marriage make me smile. My parents were obviously very much in love.

Chapter Fifteen

The Deborah Club
My mother stands on the right on the bottom
step with my father on the step behind her

The four most amazing things I learned about my father from his letters to my mother are how openly affectionate he was, how confident he was about dealing with others, how creative he was, and how fluent he was in English!

It is a testimony to his education and language skills that he could write English so well. From my own personal experience of learning French in school, I understand that writing in a foreign language is far more difficult than learning to speak and read it. In addition to English, my father also read and wrote French, and of course, German. In his letters, my father often mentions my mother "*correcting*" his English. I had to laugh because my mother continued "*correcting*" people's writing up until the day she died at age 96! She corrected the newsletters at "The Palace," the assisted living facility she lived in until her 90's. Of course, he had no idea she was a born editor—or, perhaps he did? He certainly had her figured out in 1938, a fact that was clear in his letters to her.

The earliest letter to my mother from my father is dated June 22, 1938, less than one year after he arrived in Reading, and begins, "Dearest Sylvia," and ends with, "Goodbye, honey dear! I am still with all my heart, Yours, Arthur" which surely confirms that they had not just met. That means they must have been introduced right after my father arrived in Reading in 1937. They didn't marry until January 19, 1941—a very long courtship indeed! How I wish I had a better idea of what went on in the three years they dated.

Drawing and letter Arthur wrote and sent Sylvia for the New Year, 1940

Chapter Fifteen

From his early letters, in which he suggests that she should be more optimistic and that she should not care so much what people think, I suspect my father is referring to what people are saying to my mother *about him*. It seems to have taken her a long time to commit to marriage, even though I think my parents probably fell in love with each other very quickly. My hunch is that his *"refugee"* status was probably a big part of the problem.

In America, the Jews fleeing the Nazis were referred to derisively as *"refugees,"* especially by the Russian Jews who had left their Shtetls in Ukraine in the early 1900s with only the shirts on their backs. The irony, of course, was that my mother's parents came to America with their little son Moshe and the family samovar. Period. Nothing else! When they got to Reading, they were looked down on by the German Jews who had come to the city in Pennsylvania long before them and were now landed gentry, founders and leading members of the Reform Temple. My grandparents were deeply religious Jews who helped to start the Orthodox Synagogue, and by 1937, were also settled members of the Jewish Community.

How my father felt about being looked down on by some of my mother's brothers and sisters is one of the items on that long list of things I'll never know. He was far more educated and cultured than they were, which probably intimidated them and made them pick on him even more. My father left a beautiful house, a life filled with culture and music and education, a successful tobacco business that had been in the Meier family for generations, and a loving family back in Germany. He arrived in America with a trunk full of monogrammed nightshirts, handkerchiefs, towels, table linens, and silverware.

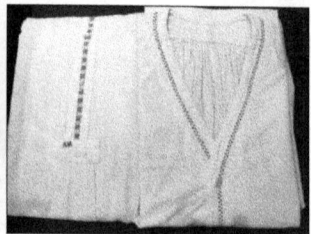

A few of the monogrammed and personal belongings that Arthur brought to America

I wonder how he dealt with people looking down on him, and I wonder how my mother ultimately persuaded herself to get into a relationship with him. I'd like to think it was the power of love.

It is a testimony to my father's remarkable resiliency that he could make a niche for himself in the hosiery industry, develop a loving relationship with my mother, make friends, and plan for the future while the news from home grew more desperately grim daily, putting him in the position of carrying around the heavy burden of what was happening to his beloved parents, family, and friends in Germany. He was a deeply sensitive, caring man. How he was able to start over is remarkable to me even all these years later.

Upon his arrival, he began to work hard on getting visas for his parents to come to the United States. The news of what his parents endured after Kristallnacht, and soon the dreadful news of them being forced to sell their house and all of its contents for a very low price in 1939, followed by their move into the newly-created "Jew House," formerly the Fetterer house on Market Square, which he knew well from his childhood and his friendship with Ernst Fetterer, must have been devastating to my father. How I wish I had asked my mother how he managed to get through all the dreadful news he was receiving constantly.

A big part of the problem of my avoidance was that I obviously and unfortunately never allowed myself to think about the timetable of the years from 1937 to 1945 in my parents' lives until it was too late to ask them about it.

The only reason I actually know when my parents finally got engaged is in the letters my grandparents sent from Germany which Martin translated. Here is the first, probably a response to a few lines my mother added to one of my father's letters to his parents.

Gengenbach, January 7, 1939

Dear Miss Sylvia!

We were very pleased with your lovely lines and we would have been even more pleased if you had introduced yourself personally. We have heard a lot of good things about you from Arthur & we are happy that he has found such a good support. We didn't know that he was attending night school in addition to all the work. Let us hope that he will continue to enjoy happiness in all his endeavors.

We hope to hear from you again, please greet your dear parents and siblings from us, learn a lot of German and be warmly greeted by Yours

Mrs & Mr Meier

Gengenbach, Januar 7. 1939

Dear Miss Sylvia!

Wir freuten uns sehr mit Ihren lieben Zeilen und noch mehr hätten wir uns gefreut, wenn Sie sich persönlich vorgestellt hätten. Wir hörten von Arthur schon viel gutes über Sie & freut es uns, dass er eine so gute Stütze an Ihnen gefunden hat. Dass er neben der vielen Arbeit auch noch die Abendschule besucht, wussten wir nicht. Wir wollen hoffen, dass ihm das Glück weiterhin in allen seinen Unternehmungen hold ist.

Wir hoffen wieder mal von Ihnen zu hören, grüßen Sie bitte Ihre lb Eltern & Geschwister von uns, lernen Sie recht viel Deutsch und seien Sie herzlichst gegrüßt von Yours

Mrs & Mr Meier

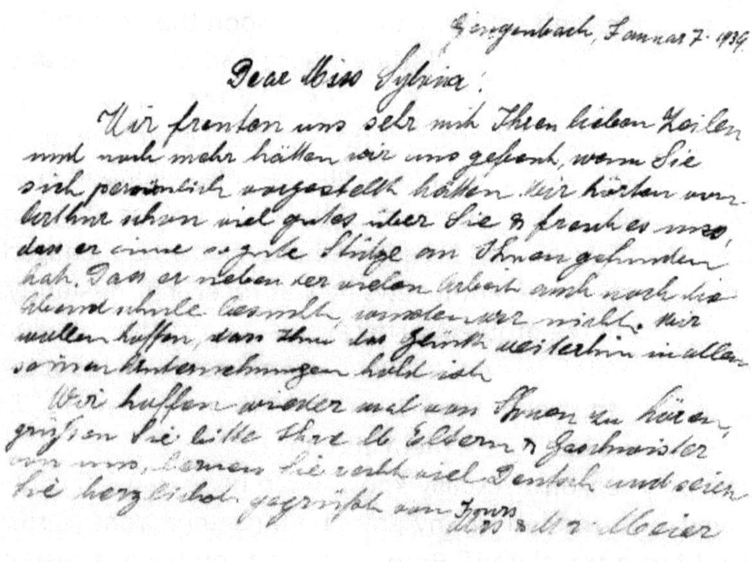

The second letter is the one to my mother after my father wrote and told his parents that he and my mother had gotten engaged.

Starting A New Life

Gengenbach, 31 August 1940

Dear Miss Sylvia!

We received your dear lines which we were very pleased to receive and we will answer them as you wish. From Arthur's lines we hear that we will soon have a daughter, which was missing until today. We are looking forward to this event and sincerely hope that you both will be happy. Arthur writes only ever enchanted and praiseworthy of you, which you have always expressed to him. For this reason, we see a happy future for both parties. Arthur has always been diligent and ambitious and popular everywhere. They also write that Arthur is gaining weight, this would not be a mistake, because judging from the pictures he looks a bit too slim, he will not allow himself enough rest. Decree a sedative to help it gain some weight. We wish you good luck and blessings, especially health, to Rosh Hashonah. May all your wishes come true.

We would like to give you something for your engagement, but unfortunately this is impossible today. Please greet your loved ones from us and be sincerely greeted by both of us.

Herr and Frau Meier

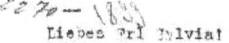

Chapter Fifteen

Sadly, their last letter, dated September 28, 1940, in which they write to Anna and David Wise who were about to become their son Arthur's in-laws, is written just weeks before their deportation to Gurs.

Gengenbach 28. September 1940

Dear Mr. & Mrs. Wise!

Yesterday we received a letter from Arthur with your daughter Sylvia's engagement announcement with our Arthur.

We warmly congratulate you on this joyful occasion and hope and wish that this connection will lead to mutual happiness. As you will be aware, our lives today are lonely and without joy, which is why the fate of our child is particularly close to us. As Arthur has written to us many times before, he has always been well received by you and therefore we have the confidence that this connection will bring our children a happy future for them.

We only have one more wish, which you will surely feel us to come back to our son when the time comes and get to know you personally at this occasion.

In our last letter, we have already sent your daughter Sylvia our congratulations in advance, which we repeat today and ask you to send Sylvia our warmest greetings.

You and all your loved ones greet you and all your loved ones warmly.

Mr. & Mrs. Berthold Meier
Congratulations belated for Rosh Hashonah

Starting A New Life

All of the letters from my father to my mother are sent from Reading where they were both living, but on April 1, 1940, the address of the letters became Lancaster, about 30 miles from Reading. There are nine letters, all written in April, from Lancaster!

Apparently, my father opened The Jeannette Hosiery Company's new store, called "Reading Mills Outlet" for someone else in Lancaster, perhaps Max Fisher. I have no idea whether or not it was related to the hosiery mill he was already working for or the business he was planning to open for himself in the near future in Pottsville.

In June 1940, the address on his letters changed again. Hosiery Mills Outlet was born on Market Street in the small town of Pottsville, Pennsylvania. This time, my father was opening his own store. It looked like a promising business as no one had yet opened a hosiery store in the town. The store caught on—selling was obviously something my father was used to and did well.

Certificate of Marriage

Arthur Meier

and

Sylvia Wise

were

United in Marriage

in Reading, PA ~~New York~~, on the 20th day of James 5701

corresponding to the 19th day of January 1941 according to the rites and usages of Israel and in conformity with the laws of the State of ~~New York~~. PA.

Max J. Routtenberg, RABBI

Henry Goldberg

WITNESSES

Chapter Fifteen

OFFICE OF REGISTER OF WILLS
and Clerk of the Orphans' Court of Berks County
in the Commonwealth of Pennsylvania

Commonwealth of Pennsylvania } ss.
County of Berks

I, _____Carl H. Savage_____ Clerk of the Orphans' Court of Berks County, do hereby certify, that _____Arthur Meier, aged 30_____ and _____Sylvia Wise, aged 25_____ were duly married on _____January 19, 1941_____; and that a return of the solemnization of said marriage is recorded in marriage Vol. __131__ No. __408__ Page __408__ as having been solemnized by _____Rabbi Max J. Routtenberg_____ on _____January 19, 1941_____

Witness my hand and seal this __26th__ day of __Sept.__ 19/60

Carl H. Savage
Clerk of Orphans' Court

Stephen S. Wanner
Asst. Clerk of Orphans' Court

My father and mother married in Reading on January 19, 1941. The only witness to their wedding still alive is my cousin Joyce. She told me that the wedding took place in my grandparents' house on Moss Street and that my mother wore a dress, not wedding gown. Considering that his parents had just been deported to Camp de Gurs in France, a more lavish affair would surely not have been appropriate. I wish I had a picture from their wedding, but none exists that I know of.

But one thing I know for sure—they planned to live happily ever after, together.

Chapter Sixteen
The Wagner-Bürckel-Aktion

October 21-22, 1940

*M*ost people have heard of Auschwitz. They have seen pictures of the camp, with its infamous sign, Arbeit Macht Frei—Work Sets You Free, standing at the entrance. While Auschwitz is well-known, the Nazis unfortunately devised many ways to kill Jews in many other places where people lived and died in circumstances far beyond comprehension. One of them was **Camp de Gurs**.

Early in Germany's attempt to rid itself of its Jews, in October 1940, The Wagner-Bürckel-Aktion sent all the Jews of the State of Baden, in the southwest part of the country near the French and Swiss borders, to a place called Camp de Gurs. Camp de Gurs was a special, personal, largely unnoticed hell in the south of France from which few people got out alive.

On November 12, 1938, two days after Kristallnacht, at a conference convened by Hermann Göring, Hitler's right-hand man and the Nazi leader who had created the Gestapo, a decree was adopted to eliminate Jews from German economic life. This effectively excluded all German Jews from the cultural life of the country. The overriding goal was to force all Jews left in Germany to emigrate, thus making the German Reich "Judenrein," "Clean of all Jews." At this conference, for the first time, plans were discussed for the deportation of German Jews to ghettos in Europe or abroad, possibly to Madagascar, an island off the coast of eastern Africa. Although many people were responsible for getting the job done, it was Adolf Eichmann who was the real power behind all of this.

In January 1939, Reinhard Heydrich was initially

Chapter Sixteen

commissioned by Göring to solve The Jewish Question by forced emigration or evacuation, the term the Nazis used to disguise what was, in fact, deportation. The Reich Central Office for Jewish Emigration was then founded under the leadership of Heydrich, who was also the head of the SD, the intelligence service.

With the signing of an armistice between the German Reich and France on June 22, 1940, the German campaign in France ended. France was divided as a result of the defeat into a German-occupied military area in the north and west of France and an unoccupied French territory in the south named the Vichy Regime. On October 4, 1940, a law was enacted in the Vichy Regime that legalized the internment of foreign Jews:

> *The Jews of foreign descent can, after this law has legal force, be interned by decision of the prefect of their residence department in special camps.*

A large number of detention camps had been built in the south of France in the spring of 1939 before the outbreak of World War II, during the Spanish Civil War, as temporary accommodations for refugees and resistance fighters fleeing Spain. One was the Camp of Barcarès in the Eastern Pyrenees, and another was the Camp of Gurs in the Western Pyrenees near the Spanish border. As a result of the war with Germany, the French government established many additional camps to intern foreign Jews and foreigners living in France who came from countries with which France was at war. These squalid and dreadful camps were sometimes euphemistically referred to as "centre d'hébergement" or "lodging centers" when the Germans spoke about them.

The Jews from Baden and the Saar Palatinate were among the first victims of Germany's new deportation plan. The initiators of The Wagner-Bürckel-Aktion, the deportation to the French internment camp at Gurs in October 1940, were two Gauleiters, district leaders, Robert Wagner of Baden and Josef Bürckel of the Saarpfalz. While it is not absolutely clear who actually first conceived of the deportation order, it was probably Himmler, the Reichsführer of the SS, who commanded this action by order of the Führer. For the Gestapo to implement the plan and the technical implementation of the trains, Wagner and Bürckel would have cooperated with Heydrich and, in particular, with Adolf Eichmann.

From the night of October 21 to the morning of October 22, 1940, at the conclusion of the Jewish Feast of Tabernacles, Succot, the German Jews of Baden and the Saar Palatinate were ordered to be ready to travel within 30 minutes to two hours. They were driven out of their homes, collected, and transported by buses and trucks staffed by the SS. The order concerned all transportable full Jews, from children to old men; there were 6,504 Germans of Jewish descent. Each person was only allowed to carry 50 kg of luggage and a cash amount of 100 Reichsmarks, and had to sign off on all goods and property left behind.

The Jews who were rounded up had no idea what the Germans had planned for them. Seven trains from Baden and two trains from the Palatinate, filled with the deportees, traveled from Germany to Vichy France. The train trip through Avignon and Toulouse lasted three days and four nights during which the Jews were fed soup only once, as they traveled southeast into France. Some Jews committed suicide in order to avoid the deportation and some older people died on the trains before reaching Gurs.

The deported people were finally loaded on trucks at the foot of the Pyrenees in Oloron-Sainte-Marie and taken to the nearby French internment camp at Gurs.

Adolf Eichmann, who had organized the transports in

Chapter Sixteen

consultation with the Reich Ministry of Transport, sat at the demarcation line in Chalon-sur-Saone, sweating in his car and watching, until the last of nine trains had crossed the border and arrived in unoccupied France. Reinhard Heydrich noted with satisfaction that the deportations ran smoothly and without incident and were hardly noticed by the population. On October 23, Robert Wagner reported to Berlin that his district was the first district of the empire to be "Judenrein," "Free of all Jews."

The detention center at Gurs was completely unprepared for the arrival of some 6000 deportees. Due to the dreadful supply situation, the catastrophic hygienic conditions, and the rain and cold, many deportees died soon after their arrival at Camp de Gurs. Some of the German Jews who survived were eventually distributed to neighboring camps: Noé Detention Center, Le Vernet, Les Milles, Rivesaltes, and Récébédou. The conditions at Gurs were considered to be the worst in all of the camps.

The deportees were helpless and destitute in the foreign land. The Madagascar Plan was still in force, and the deportees were still to be sent to Madagascar immediately after the opening of the sea routes. The Swedish Foreign Ministry suggested the issuing of passports to the deportees to immigrate to South America. From 1941 on, some of the Jews succeeded, with the help of international aid organizations and personal contacts, to immigrate to safe third countries. Many did not. The number of visas issued to immigrate to America was very limited and slow to achieve because of the strong anti-immigrant and anti-Semitic sentiment among many American citizens. Some people were issued visas after they had already been sent off to their deaths, too late to take advantage of the ability to travel *to safety.*

When the Vichy Regime repeatedly complained about the unannounced transport of Jews and demanded a directive on facts and instructions from the German side in a protest note to the Franco-German Armistice Commission in Wiesbaden, Reich Foreign Minister Joachim von Ribbentrop ordered the request for information to be dismissed. The Federal Foreign Office made no fundamental criticism of the deportations themselves but demanded participation in the decision-making process in the future. It was decided to take foreign policy considerations into account to coordinate ongoing deportation measures.

The Wagner-Bürckel-Aktion on October 22, 1940 was the first of its kind in the Third Reich. The smooth interaction of different authorities in the planning and implementation in these early deportations of Jews was a testimony to German efficiency. It led, after the fact, to complaints about diplomatic and political complications, but this meant little to the more than 6,000 victims of the Aktion and their families.

The deportation of the Jews from Baden and the Saar Palatinate to Gurs in France was one of the earliest deportations before the summer of 1941. The Aktion was a financial success, netting the German government over 60 million confiscated Reichsmarks and much property, making the deportation to Gurs a self-paying and profitable venture. On July 31, 1941, inspired by the success of this plan, Hermann Göring began building concentration camps, and he instructed Reinhard Heydrich the architect of the Final Solution to make preparations to end The Jewish Question once and for all in the German sphere of influence in Europe.

In August 1942, after the Germans took over the Vichy Regime, a newly-created plan dictated that the 3,907

Chapter Sixteen

Jews who were still alive in the detention camps in the south of France were to be sent systematically, by trains, at the request of Theodor Dannecker, an Eichmann Commissioner, to the camp at Drancy near Paris, well within sight of the beautiful city.

Those Jews who lived through the trip to Drancy were then to be sent east to German extermination camps—most of them to Auschwitz-Birkenau and Maidanek-Sobibor—Göring's prized creations. Thus, within two years, the National Socialists in Nazi Germany had in fact succeeded in achieving the Total Solution of The Jewish Question with their earliest victims, the Jews of Baden.

The only positive note in this tragic story is that both Wagner and Bürckel paid for their crimes against the Jews of Baden. Bürckel committed suicide on November 8, 1944, and Wagner was executed by a French firing squad on August 8, 1946. Unfortunately, these men could only die once, not nearly sufficient payment for the countless victims they killed and lives they affected, and still do.

Among the victims of The Wagner-Bürckel-Aktion were Sophie and Berthold Meier of Gengenbach, my grandparents, and many of their relatives and friends. The early story of Camp de Gurs, largely unmentioned in stories and movies about the Nazis and their evil sins, is greatly in need of becoming a better-known chapter in the history of the Holocaust.

PHILADELPHIA RECORD, SATURDAY, DECEMBER 28, 1940

12,000 Facing Starvation In French Refugee Camp

By STEVE FULTON

NEW YORK, Dec. 27 (UP)—Some 12,000 refugees, including 6000 Jews uprooted on one hour's notice from their German homes, are existing on rations sufficient for only 8000 to 9000 persons in the big French concentration camp at Gurs, in the Pyrenees Mountains, near the Spanish border.

That is the information given me on my homeward trip from Vichy by a Portuguese Red Cross official, F. Sahlman, who had just made an inspection of the camp.

"I went to the Gurs camp," Sahlman said, "to see for myself how living conditions were, and I was shocked at the housing problems. In one small shack without windows and virtually without ventilation I found 150 people.

Many Doomed to Die.

"The food situation is far from satisfactory. It is understandable that the French cannot do any more for these people than for their own. But there could be some improvement.

"When 6000 German Jewish refugees arrived from the Palatinate, Baden and Wurtemberg, the commander of the camp received no increase in his food allowance. If this situation continues many of the older refugees, as well as the sick and some 500 children, will die for lack of nourishment."

Sahlman said the Jews were given only an hour's notice to pack a few belongings and leave Germany.

Letter Smuggled Out.

Sahlman had obtained a letter, smuggled out of the camp, telling of the plight of the Jewish refugees.

It said:

"On the morning of October 22 Jews from the Saar Palatinate, the Palatinate, the Grand Duchy of Baden and the Wurtemberg rovince were awakened by the Gestapo and warned to be ready to leave Germany within one hour.

"They were informed they would be allowed to carry with them 100 reichsmarks and 110 pounds of luggage.

"Aged persons, some 80 and 90 years old, as well as sick and feeble men and women, were among those deported.

54-Hour Train Ride.

"After a 54-hour train ride, during which soup was given us only once, we arrived at a station in the Basses Pyrenees department. From there we were taken to the Gurs camp in trucks.

"Owing to the fact that the French commander of the Gurs camp had not been advised as to our number and was taken by surprise by our mass arrival, it is not astonishing that he lacked food at the beginning. Despite the fact that the French Administration are doing all it can to help the internees, it is understandable that old people and the sick cannot resist the hardships of camp life.

"During the few weeks of our stay here at Gurs the camp cemetery has grown in an anguishing proportion."

Gurs was used before the war to house Spanish Republicans who fled Spain after the Franco victory. The camp is built of wooden huts. Many are obliged to sleep on the bare floor. Mattresses and blankets are lacking despite the cold weather.

---

obtained, and that further imprisonment will work no beneficial result."

Brownmiller, a resident of Pottsville, was convicted here July 25, 1939, on two counts of allowing a padded payroll among his departmental workers. The trial was the result of campaign charges.

Entered Prison in October.

Brownmiller was sentenced October 16, 1939, and released in $10,000 bail pending an appeal to higher courts. Last September 11 the State Supreme Court dismissed the appeal and Brownmiller surrendered to begin his term October 28.

When Judge Hughes sentenced Bownmiller, he told him:

"We realize you received no personal gain through the misuse of your office."

Of several Democrats indicted, Brownmiller was the only one sentenced to jail.

Friends Help Pay.

Friends of Brownmiller contributed to pay his fine and costs. It was understood he would go to work for P. J. McCall, Lansford, president of the Mary-D Coal Mining Company. McCall, at a hearing before Judge Hughes, said he offered Brownmiller the sales managership of the concern.

NAZI FILMS RULED HATRED FOMENTERS

LOS ANGELES, Dec. 27 (UP)—Showing of German-made motion pictures, however innocent the purpose, is a "means for fomenting hatred, criticism and enmity," the Superior Court held today in upholding the right to two theater owners to cancel a lease.

The theater proprietors, Dr. Peter Riccardi and Roger Rogers, canceled the lease which permitted Frank K. Ferenz use of their theater. They charged he exhibited German propaganda in films furnished at no cost by the German consul.

BRITISH FINISHING LETTER TO HITLER

Chapter Seventeen

Bonbons from Herr Meier

October 22, 1940

It was Annemie Sewald's job to go to the bakery each morning to get bread for her family's breakfast. The smell of fresh bread always made her rush home after buying it. But this morning, as she was walking toward her house with the delicious-smelling bread in her basket, she saw something happening in front of Hauptstraße 4, the Judenhaus—the Jew House—which made her stop. There was an Army truck parked by the door. A Gestapo officer was standing, watching several old Jewish people exit the house and struggle to climb into the truck, each carrying what appeared to be a very heavy suitcase. As she watched, she realized that the man who had just come through the door, headed for the truck, carrying a suitcase, was her friend, Herr Meier, the tobacco merchant. Herr Meier was dearly loved by all the children of the village for the wonderful bonbons he always had for them.

Annemie had overheard her parents talking about how he and the other Jewish men in Gengenbach had been sent somewhere called Dachau for a short time after the trouble in 1938. Herr Meier came back to Gengenbach, but after that he didn't pay any attention to the children. He didn't give out bonbons anymore. After he and his wife had to sell their house on Grünstraße and move into the Judenhaus on Hauptstraße with the Valfer and Fetterer families, she didn't see him much.

When Annemie recognized Herr Meier, she inched her way closer to the truck. She heard the SS officer laugh and say, "Where you're going you won't need those," pointing to the shiny German Army World War I medals on Herr Meier's coat. The officer reached over and ripped them off, one by one. Annemie saw them fall and scatter all over the ground. Herr Meier looked down at the falling medals and then at his coat where they had been only moments earlier. He looked at the Gestapo officer and then silently began to help the woman standing behind him climb

Chapter Seventeen

into the truck, pushing her heavy bag up to her. After she was in, pulling his own load behind him, he struggled into the truck. The officer made no attempt to help him.

Moments later, Annemie watched as the truck drove slowly away from the house. When it had turned the corner, she walked over to where it had stood. She saw the medals lying on the ground. Holding the basket with the now-cold bread carefully so it wouldn't fall, she reached down and picked up Herr Meier's bent and broken medals and put them in her coat pocket. Then she walked home.

The boy wearing the cap coming through the gate with his bag is Kurt Maier. This photo was taken in Kippenheim as the Jews were loaded onto SS trucks taking them to the nearest railway station at Offenburg to await boarding the train to Gurs.

Chapter Eighteen
Early Letter from Gurs

When I read the translation of this letter from Martin, I spent days bumping into walls—grief-stricken. My grandfather's early letter, written on January 4, 1941 from Gurs to my father, came as a shock to me—both what it said and the emotion with which it was written. Reading the translation of it was one of the most difficult things I've ever done. I had never "heard" Berthold Meier's "voice" before and the despair in it broke my heart. I can't even begin to imagine what it must have been like for my father to read this letter.

Berthold Meier
Ilot E Baraque 25
Camp de Gurs
Basses Pyrénées
4. Januar 1941

Dear Arthur! We received your letter from the 9. 12 after long waiting, finally, on the 18. 1. 41. Now I waited since that time for other news, however, nothing came till this day. What I particularly expected, some money, would be necessary to be able to buy something to the inadequate food. Till this day we have some money, but on the length it is not enough. Most have already received money and food. We received from no side till this day something. The different was informed by Berte Dissenhufen. 1 coat, shoes, food, and by a representative who came here 10 fr for mummy hand over, these were not delivered and mummy received from the other things only coat which nevertheless 3 weeks was in the possession of another Meier, these are 4 same names in the Ilot J. I have complained to the post whether successfully is doubtful. Uncle Adolf let by his daughter from Nice also money + send food, nevertheless, nothing came till this day. If we were at home on the green in Müller Karls house at the back under the floor, we would be much better. How long we it endure so is a question. I can visit mummy

Chapter Eighteen

all 14 days on 1 hour. We are in the dirt, it is indescribable in what we must take part and how long still it will last? I have soon lost the faith that we can come to you, rather I think if it goes on in such a way that we can decide our life still here.

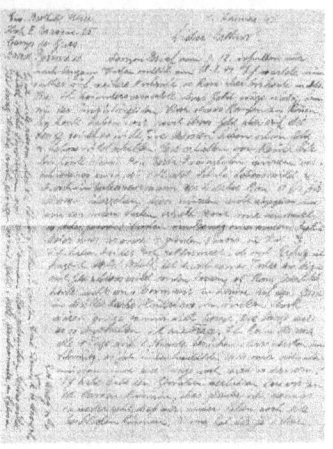

(Notice at side): It is not to be sent advisable about the Swiss things. A company R. H. Marcy explains such things. We can use everything, food, clothes, laundry, also carried as well as money. Many congratulations to Sylvia.

On your question what we took from at home says you, only that what I could carry and wore. I bought to myself here already an old suit, working trousers, a pullover and 1 pair of slippers, so that spares my things, I have taken only one good suit. We have already nothing. What we, however, mostly need money is for food, because in the morning + in the evening black Kafe, at noon a soup is not to live, in addition daily ¼ kg of bread what one could eat all at once. If something can allow, some money sends us monthly. There are also by relief organizations maps, turn you, nevertheless, to such. From Bertell we have nothing, neither money nor food receive, they have lied to you. Our things at home will be auctioned long ago, asks for sometimes with Helmut. Mummy always says, your letters are without love, more according to business written. Uncle Adolf has the old address. After G. let by Berta write, but still nothing preserved. If you write to us, nevertheless, also adds, like others, an international reply coupon, because 1,4 ½ fr is for us money. You can write everything openly. In the meantime, you will have closed with Sylvia the marriage, I could not send our Jewish names you on time, you could have done this long ago before, I have asked for with you earlier what you needs in papers. Seriously and Johanna, also Gretel Valfer are still in Germany because only Baden and the Palatinate were expelled. Now you know what we lack. Help so well you are able and takes steps to our emigration, enquires you with Bertel.

With the heartiest greetings your father

Early Letter from Gurs

(Notice at side): Yes, dear Arthur, so is our situation, we would be glad if we had only enough bread. This letter has hidden again with the post when your today's letter just arrived from the 28.12. Our number is 29908. My Jewish name Jesoschor, from mummy Sorle. It is with us in such a way as you have read.

In shock I read one line over and over—*If we were at home on the green in Müller Karl's house at the back under the floor, we would be much better.* My grandfather was saying that he would be better off back in Gengenbach, in his old home *under the floor*—of the house he was born in, lived in for 50 years, and had to "sell" to Karl Lambrecht in 1939 when all Jews had to give up their properties, than he was at Gurs. *I have soon lost the faith that we can come to you, rather I think if it goes on in such a way that we can decide our life still here.* His premonition that he would never make it to America

Chapter Eighteen

is frightening. And pitiful. His description of the conditions at Gurs—the lack of food, the filth, what they need just to live—is accurate. A year later my grandmother, his wife, would die of starvation.

Ah, but a man who was on his way to hell, literally—but who was still a father—passing on the message that Arthur's mother thought his letters were too cold and business-like. And then my grandfather ended by chewing my father out for not asking for his parents' Hebrew names in time for his wedding to my mother! Just like a father would do under normal circumstances!

This was my first real glimpse of my grandfather. He wrote so clearly and honestly, so simply but realistically, that I suddenly felt as though I was finally really meeting him. I could almost hear him scolding my father!

What a paradox this translated letter presented me with—it reminded me of the painful facts I had not learned all the years I was in avoidance and how hurtful the truth was to me now that I was facing it. On the other hand, I realized that I had gotten a gift—I had finally found my grandfather!

Chapter Nineteen

What's in a Name?

It has long been a Jewish custom to name a newborn child after a deceased relative. It is a special way of honoring an ancestor. That means that, over time, a lot of Jewish children were given the biblical or ethnic name of a grandparent or other family member who had died. That custom has been pretty consistent over the ages, right up to today. Therefore, there still are lots of little Jewish kids named Max or Leo or Julia or Sarah, just as there always were.

However, there was a break with that tradition for a time among American Jews. In an attempt to make their children sound genuinely American during the Holocaust, most Jewish parents during those years chose girls' names like Susan, Carol, Debbie, Judy, and similar ethnically-clean American names. The boys became Mark, Bruce, Robert, or Michael. Therefore, most of my friends born in the 1940s were given American-sounding names. You won't find too many American Jewish adults my age who are named Sophie. Or Bertha, Rosa, Alfred or Samuel.

When I was born on December 24, 1942, my German grandmother, Sophie Roland Meier, had been dead for only eleven months. My parents, Sylvia and Arthur, wanted to name me after her. That should have made my name *Sophie Roland Meier*, but it didn't—not in 1942! Instead of Sophie, I was named Susan and instead of Roland I was given a middle name that began with an "R" that I hated so much that the minute I married for the first time I got rid of it and became Susan Meier Moss. Unless you read my birth certificate, you will never know what my real middle name is!

In addition to an English name, Jewish children are also given a Hebrew name. That name is used for ceremonial events such as a Bris, Bar or Bat Mitzvah, wedding, or funeral—times when you are linked with your parents. I am *Shoshana bat (daughter of) Asher and Zipporah*. My parents named me *Shoshana*, supposedly my Grandma Sophie's Hebrew name, a pretty name

Chapter Nineteen

that I have always loved and used proudly. However, I recently discovered, when it came to my Hebrew name, my parents somehow messed that up, too, a fact I didn't know until I read my grandfather's first letter from Gurs!

When Martin Ruch translated and emailed me the translation of an early letter my grandfather sent to my father shortly after he got to Gurs, I was terribly overwhelmed reading about the train trip from Offenburg to Gurs and the dreadfully inadequate food, clothing and shelter that my grandparents found in their new French quarters.

I was so saddened reading my grandfather's pathetic wish to be back home under the floor in his old house that I missed something very important—the note in the margin.

Among other things, there was a shortage of paper for letter-writing at Gurs, and often there were short messages written in the margins of letters.

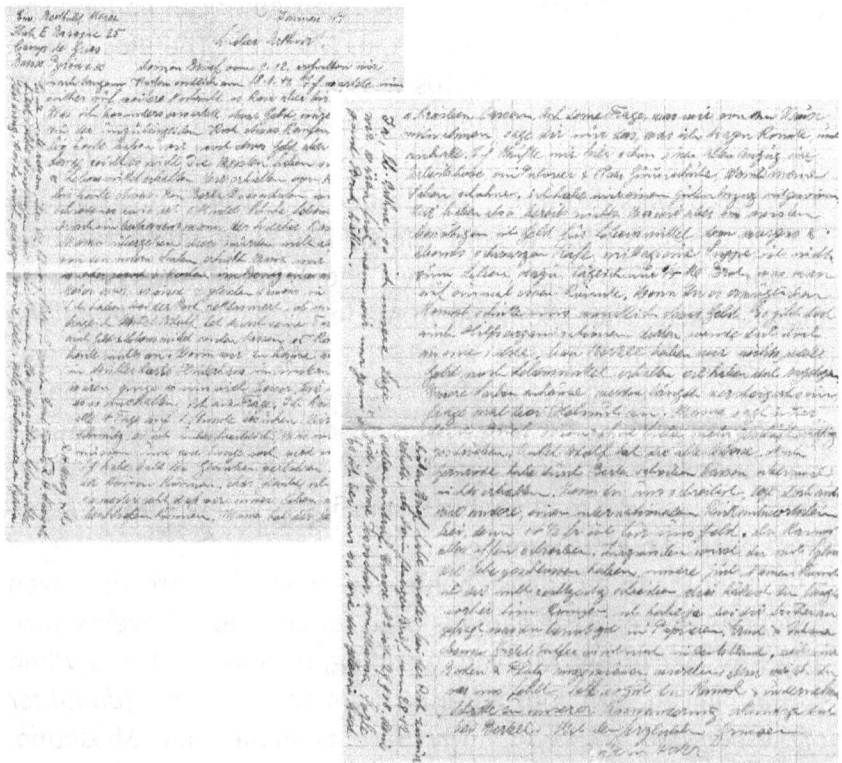

Lieber Arthur!
...Du kannst alles offen schreiben. Inzwischen wirst du mit Sylvia die Ehe geschlossen haben, unsere jüdischen Namen konnte ich dir nicht rechtzeitig schicken, dies hättest du längst vorher tun können, ich habe ja bei dir früher angefragt, was du benötigst in Papieren.

Mein jüd. Name Jesoschor, von Mama Sorle.
Mit den herzlichsten Grüssen Dein Vater

Dear Arthur,
You can write anything openly. In the meantime, you will have married Sylvia. I could not send our Jewish names to you on time. You could have done this long ago before. I asked you what papers you needed.

My Jewish Name Jesoschor, from Mama Sorle.
With the warmest greetings
Your Father

Recently when I reread Martin's translation of that first letter from Gurs written by my grandfather on January 4, 1941, I found the surprise that lurked in the margin, where my grandfather refers to my parents' impending wedding, about to take place in January 1941.

My grandfather gives my father hell for not asking for his parents' Hebrew names sooner so they could be used in the wedding. And then he supplies the missing names. He says, *My Hebrew name is Jesoschor and Mama's Hebrew name is Sorle. Sorle!* NOT *Shoshana!*

How my parents got from *Sorle* to *Shoshana* is lost to the ages. Since my father was the only one of my parents who read German, I guess he is the one to blame—my mother, Sylvia, is innocent, I think.

It is a little late now at age 80 to change either of my names, English or Hebrew, don't you think? A little too late to become *Sophie Roland Meier* or even *Sorle...*

Sorry, Grandma...

Chapter Twenty
Pottsville: The Early Years
1941-1947

My parents began married life together in Pottsville. They moved into an apartment on Norwegian Street and quickly made friends. My father began to be successful with his new business on Market Street.

In front of Hosiery Mills Outlet on Market Street, my father's store

Much to his delight, my father found other Germans in Pottsville. Karl and Lassia Spitzer were an older couple who came from Berlin where Karl had been a judge. Wonderfully creative, Karl was the artist who drew the beautiful postcard we received when my mother and I were visiting my father in South Carolina in 1944.

Closer in age to my father was Simon Hammel, who ran the Pottsville branch of the Ehrlich Exterminating Company. Simon

Chapter Twenty

and my father became close friends, sharing similar backgrounds, which must have been special for both of them.

Life was good in Pottsville—but, through it all, the news from Germany continued to get worse. Despite my father's efforts to help his parents in Gurs, his mother, Sophie, died of starvation on January 13, 1942. A sad message from his father reached my father sometime later. By the time he got the terrible news, she had already been dead and buried for a time, so he asked my Orthodox Grandmother Wise what he should do. "Sit Shiva," she told him. So he did.

My mother became pregnant in March of 1942 and the young couple eagerly awaited their baby, me, due in December. I've always wondered if they decided to have a baby before or after my father got word of his mother's death.

My father worked frantically on getting a visa for his father from the State Department. My mother's former boss from Reading, Sam Brown, the owner of National Window Cleaning, co-sponsored the visa requests, but the US immigration policy was against the efforts my father was making.

Today, knowing how hard my father was trying to get visas for his parents, I find it frustrating to read the letters my father received from various relatives on his mother's side of the family which Martin translated for me, urging him to do more for his parents, regularly laying a guilt trip on him in each letter. He was frantically working on getting his father out of France, but his bad luck and the low number of visas issued continued to be a problem.

In October 1942, Berthold Meier's visa for travel to the United States was finally issued! My father sent a telegram to let his father know the good news, but the Germans occupied Vichy France on November 10, 1942, so my father never knew if his father got the telegram. Berthold Meier disappeared and was never heard from again. Arthur never knew what happened to his father. The information about what happened to Berthold Meier only became available many years later. Ironically, it was not until the year 2000 that I became the first family member to learn the truth about Transport 50 to Maidanek/Sobibor.

In the middle of all these tragedies, I was born on December 24, 1942. My father was thrilled with his new little daughter. My parents named me Susan after my grandmother, Sophie.

As if it was not hard enough to live in a new country, start a new life, build a business, get citizenship, and start a family, Arthur Meier proved unsuccessful at avoiding being drafted.

Chapter Twenty

My father became an American citizen on May 25, 1943, and immediately received his draft notice from the U.S. Army. He desperately tried to get out of having to join, but with no luck. He had no choice but to turn the business over to my mother, and, after completing his basic training on January 19, 1944, when I was a one-year-old, he was sent to Columbia, South Carolina to translate in the prisoner of war camp for German soldiers at Ft. Jackson—to translate German into English for men who had been fighting for the Nazis only months earlier!

My mother, of course, was left to run Hosiery Mills Outlet. That meant that, in addition to being the mother of a one-year-old, she had to go into the store each day to run the business and sell. She also had to go on buying trips to get new merchandise, so I had a nanny named Martha Harhigh. I remember Martha singing me the song, "St. Louis," which began "Meet me in St. Louis, Louis, meet me at the Fair..." I was also the darling of the salesladies in the store and so, was very well cared for even though my mother told me I missed my father very much.

It is not common knowledge that German prisoners of war were brought to the U.S., but they were. Using German Jewish men to act as translators in prisoner of war camps in the United States was also a very common thing for the military to do. There was a shortage of translators, what better translator than a man who had been German until recently, sometimes as little as a few months separating the man's two nationalities! Apparently, the process did not always go smoothly—resentment was clearly understandable on both sides as many of the German prisoners saw Jews as translators to be an affront and the Jews resented the soldiers for what the Germans were doing back home in Germany to their families.

My father appeared to have avoided this issue. He got along with the German prisoners very well. My mother told me that he used the German doctor in the camp when he was sick, and when she warned him that the doctor could kill him, he laughed at her and told her not to worry. Apparently, that wasn't how it was for him with the prisoners either—I have several lovely things the German soldiers made as gifts for him, among them a beautiful still-life painting that hangs in my living room and an inlaid wooden cigar box one prisoner made for him.

My father, seated in the front row on the right, with other soldiers at Ft. Jackson

I was only a year old when my father left Pottsville to go into the Army. In June 1945 my mother and I took a train to South Carolina to see him.

The postcard Karl Spitzer made and sent us

Chapter Twenty

I vaguely remember the apartment we stayed in during that visit. I have often looked at the picture of my mother and me in front of the white columns of the very southern-looking house. I once dragged poor Irwin around Columbia, South Carolina for hours looking for it, but sixty years later, the house with the columns was nowhere to be found. Of course, it might have helped if I had had an address!

My father even wrote to me while he was away. I still have the letter he wrote to me for my second birthday in 1944. I have read it on every birthday I have had since and treasure the good luck and inspiration that brought it to me all those years ago, and still does.

> December 12, 1944
>
> Dear Susan,
>
> Was it with Martha's support, or did Martha have yours when you sent me this nice letter.
>
> Susan, you tell Martha that I enjoyed reading it very much. I was sorry when you invited me to your birthday party, because I know that I will never be able to make it. Thanks anyhow for inviting me, and also for that sweet letter.
>
> Now, honey, you will be 2 years old, and are becoming a little lady. It just seems like yesterday when you were laying in your little crib, took your botty, and cried maaa..., and it was'nt on time. Then you started out on your feet in the play pen, and today you are running around like a grown-up girl. Look, how fast you are growing up, soon you will be going to school.
>
> Pappy would like to see all these new tricks, Mamma tells me about.
>
> I am glad to hear that you are a good child, eat good, and like to play with your toys.
>
> Tell Martha to take you to Santa Claus if Mammie is busy, and to make a big birthday party for you, and to invite all your friends.
>
> Yes, snookie, I miss you very much. But if it cannot be for your birthday, Pappy will see you right after Christmas. He can hardly wait till that time arrives.
>
> Will you excuse me, when I cannot be present at your party. I hope that Mammie, Martha and you will have a very good time without me too, and that next year at this time I shall be with you all.
>
> It's cold here also, but up there I think it's worse yet. Do you have snow? I think you should wish yourself a sleigh for your birthday, and Martha should take you out. That will be lots of fun for you.
>
> I am wishing you, dear Susan, a happy birthday, and many more. You should become a healthy and successful daughter, and have happiness during a long, great life.
>
> And to Mammie and Martha you always must listen, and be thankful.
>
> Say hello to Mammie and Martha, and tell them they should take good care of you, and show you a good time.
>
> Here is a big kiss from
>
> yours
>
> *Pappy*

While he did not seem to experience the issues that many Jewish translators did, the conflicting feelings he had still must have been very difficult for him. The trauma he experienced in Germany between 1933 and 1937 must have resonated in him. In addition to hating the Army, my father was also dealing with the fact that despite his attempts to get a visa for his father, HIAS could not do anything further until Berthold Meier could be found. He was already dead, a sad fact my father did not yet know. Arthur was diagnosed with high blood pressure and a heart condition by the time he got out of the Army on December 6, 1945.

Chapter Twenty

When my father returned to Pottsville from the Army, my parents moved up the hill to a larger apartment on a street with an interesting Native American name—"Mahantongo" Street! The address to which they moved was two houses away from the birthplace of the famous writer, John O'Hara; the setting of many of O'Hara's books was, in fact, Pottsville. Also down Mahantongo Street was a famous brewery with another interesting name—Yuengling!

Several dozen Jewish men from Pottsville drafted during World War II formed a large group of Jewish War Veterans when they returned home. My father is in the third row from the front, the last man standing on the right.

I was thrilled to have my father back home. We started doing things together, a custom that continued for the rest of his life. Simon Hammel and his wife Ernestine had a little boy named Victor. I remember banging pots and pans on the Hammel's kitchen floor while visiting them.

Spending time in my father's store was one of my greatest delights. I think, looking back, that I pretended I was selling hosiery to the customers. In those days, ladies' stockings were beautifully packaged, meticulously folded by the manufacturer, and boxed, several matching pairs per slim container. I loved taking the boxes off the shelves and opening the lids. My father repeatedly cautioned me not to touch the actual stockings. He and the salesladies had learned how to put their hands into the delicate hosiery to show customers how that particular shade looked. I couldn't do that as I might have put a pull into the delicate nylons. When I lost interest in playing saleslady, I went to the office in the back of the store where my father had a typewriter that he allowed me to use. I can still close my eyes today and remember the feel of the metal rims of the keys, which all early typewriters had, on my fingers as I typed away. Typewriters were so special to me that I had trouble making the switch to computers when they came into my life early in the 1990s. Today, I would kill anyone who tried to take my computer away from me, but it took a long time for me to give up my love of typewriters, developed at an early age in the office at Hosiery Mills Outlet in the 1940s.

I wish I could tell you that my father survived his stint in the Army and came back to success when he got out, but I can't. He didn't know it yet, but he had missed out on the cream at the top of the bottle of the hosiery business during World War II. Just as he came home to the north, the hosiery business began to move south.

My mother became pregnant for a second time in September 1946. Although I had been an only child for a long time, I was excited at the idea of having a baby sister or brother. I was sent to Reading to stay with my Aunt Julia and Uncle Herman when my mother was about to give birth. After a few days, I got tired of waiting for the phone call from my father that a baby had been born, so I told Aunt Julia's next door neighbor that my mother had had a baby. She came running over to congratulate my aunt, only to learn that I had made the story up!

On June 20th, my father finally called to tell me that I had

Chapter Twenty

a baby brother and that they were going to name him Jeffrey Bruce. I immediately reacted by saying that I didn't like the name Bruce. "What do you like better?" my father asked me, surprised. I was, after all, only 4½ years old. My father was a pretty definite man, and it was not like him to ask others' opinions. I think I had shocked him into asking me.

"Burton," I immediately said. "Jeffrey Burton Meier."

And that is my brother's name—Jeffrey <u>Burton</u> Meier. It sounds much more distinguished than Jeffrey <u>Bruce</u> Meier, but where in heaven's name did I get the name "Burton!?"

We were now a family of four, just a bit crowded on Mahantongo Street

Chapter Twenty-One

Pottsville: The House on 22nd Street

1948-1954

*I*n 1948, when Jeffrey was a year old and I was five years old, just in time for me to start first grade, we moved to what could technically be called "the suburbs" of Pottsville. The town was so small that all it meant was that we lived 22 blocks from the downtown where my father's store was located. The white, semi-detached house my parents bought at 15 North 22nd Street was one of a row of four sets of semi-detached houses on a very steep hill. The neighbors on our other half were the Diamond family.

At the front of each house was a large, square front porch. Ours had a metal glider with soft cushions that we often sat on. The other thing on the front porch was the silver aluminum milk box. Each day, the milkman came in his truck and delivered whatever you asked for in the note you left him. He also took the empty milk bottles. The box was insulated, so you could get dairy products delivered all year round.

Along the side of the house was a narrow driveway which widened at the end and led to a double garage. Ours was the tiny one-car garage on the right. The Yoffe's, our neighbors across the driveway, owned the tiny one on the left. In those days, few families owned more than one car, so a one-car garage was just fine.

The house was not big, but it was four stories high, with wooden floors on the first and second floors and on the stairs. Even the attic had a wooden floor. Only the kitchen and basement floors were different—the kitchen had a floor covered in what used to be called "linoleum" and the basement had a concrete floor.

On the first floor was the front porch, the living room with a fake fireplace, the dining room, and the kitchen. There was a back door in the kitchen which led to a small porch with three steps that led down to the back yard.

Chapter Twenty-One

Jeffrey and I sitting on the back porch

The second floor had three bedrooms and a bathroom, connected by a hallway. My parents' room was to the right when you got to the top of the stairs, and it faced the street. My brother's room and the bathroom faced the driveway, and my room at the back faced the back yard and the farmer's field beyond the stone wall at the end of our yard.

It was an interesting house. If you looked up while standing in the hallway on the second floor, you saw a door in the ceiling—really—a door in the ceiling with a chain hanging from where the doorknob should have been! If you pulled on the chain, the door swung down, and a set of steps slid down until they rested on the hallway floor. Because there was also a basement in the house, these steps led to what should technically have been called the attic or fourth floor. But we called it the "third floor." The walls of the third floor were not finished, but it was clean and dry and had several windows for light.

All of my father's treasures from Germany—including the large steamer trunk which had traveled with him on the train across the Rhine River, leading to Strasbourg, France and then to Paris, and finally, by ship to America with him—now lived on the third floor. It was filled with what he had brought with him from his enchanted childhood and his family. As a child I had no idea that because my father would leave us so early in our lives, his belongings would become one of the most important ways we would have of remembering him.

The green photo album and the stamp collection, the most treasured things of all, lived on the third floor in the changing table my brother and I had outgrown. It is with deep regret that I think about the green photo album in the changing table. It didn't get lost. My mother kept it after my father died. I still have it. I have even created a beautiful book from the photo album. My regret comes from the fact that I didn't ask my father who the unknown people in the pictures were. I didn't ask their names or how they figured in his life. I didn't ask, and he didn't volunteer.

Since I was not tall enough to reach the chain nor strong enough to pull it down to open the steps, I only got to go up to the third floor when one of my parents did. It was my father whom I remember most as being the person on the third floor with me, mostly I guess because of his German stamp collection. My father often went up to look at it, and he continued to add to it whenever he could get a new German stamp.

Among the treasures in the steamer trunk were my father's violin and his mandolin, still in their cases. I never saw him look at nor heard him play either of the instruments he had been lovingly playing with skill since he was a young boy. Perhaps, having left his home behind the way he had to, he found it too painful to play them anymore.

My father still loved music, however. We had a beautiful piece of wooden furniture, a Magnavox radio and record player, in the living room on which my father played his records or the radio regularly. Most of the music my father listened to on his beloved record player was classical—some symphonies in big albums that contained multiple records—some on as many as four records—eight sides—from beginning to end. My father had a great sense of fun, and he played polkas and marches while he and Jeffrey and I marched around the house, using pots and pans and wooden spoons to bang with as we listened to John Phillip Sousa's "Stars and Stripes Forever." I cannot listen to a Sousa march even today without smiling, remembering the joy we shared together to that music. Although he was in my life for such a short time, my

Chapter Twenty-One

father succeeded at instilling his love of music in me. To this day, one of my great joys in life remains classical music.

My father was very, very strict, but the only fights I actually remember having with him were over practicing the piano. We had an upright piano in the dining room which my mother played. My parents decided to give me piano lessons. I was intrigued about playing, but I hated the teacher, and I hated practicing. After a couple of major fights with my father, my piano lessons ended very abruptly. I regret it to this day—and my favorite classical music is still piano concertos!

We called the basement "the cellar." We didn't count it as a floor of the house. You got to the cellar, which had a concrete floor and walls, by going down steps that were behind a door nestled between the living and dining rooms.

The basement had a coal furnace and a coal bin which held the coal for the furnace. The coal bin was a little room that had high wooden walls with only an opening wide enough to take the coal out with a shovel. It had a high window in it that opened into the driveway. When the coal bin was getting empty, my parents ordered a coal delivery. A truck would drive into our driveway, open the window of the coal bin, put in a chute that led from the truck into the window, and send coal down the chute into our coal bin.

When that happened, my brother and I loved sitting in the dining room and looking out of the window which was just above the one that led to the coal bin. We loved watching the black and shiny anthracite, a hard coal mined in nearby towns, slide down the chute. We loved watching the coal being delivered, but, thinking back to the work my father or mother had to do to shovel the coal into the furnace daily, I realize it was not quite as romantic as it seemed to us.

Besides putting coal into the furnace, my parents had to clean up the ashes left over after the coal burned. The ashes had to be cleaned out of the bottom of the furnace and put into a metal garbage can that I guess somebody came and collected, although I have no memory of what happened after the ashes went into the garbage can. All in all, it must have been a dreadful job for my parents, one that lasted all winter.

The basement also had a primitive washing machine with a wringer attached that my mother had to use to get enough water out of the clothes so she could hang them up to dry. I don't know if clothes dryers had been invented yet in the 1940's, but we didn't have one. Putting heavy, wet laundry though that wringer must have been a very hard job. In winter, my mother, wearing a coat to keep warm—there was no heat in the cellar— hung the clothes with clothespins on a clothesline in the cellar. In summer, she hung them from a clothesline in the back yard. In those days, if you hung your laundry outside to dry, you would end up with delicious-smelling, warm laundry, dried by the sun. Honestly, hard as it is to believe, this was true once upon a time!

My father also stored paint and paint brushes on wooden shelves near the back door of the basement, which had steps that led up to the back yard. He always seemed to be painting some part of the house, listening to the baseball game, mostly to the Philadelphia Phillies, on the radio as he worked. I have a very vivid memory of my brother and I hanging around him while he painted. He always seemed to enjoy himself as he kept busy, a trait Jeffrey and I both inherited.

My other vivid memory, besides seeing the third floor treasures and painting the house, is the garden. My father grew vegetables and flowers, which he planted each spring and which he tended to with skill. I did not yet know, of course, that his home in Germany had gardens in the front and on the sides, including his grandfather's beautiful pear trees. I did not know that this was something he was used to—planting and tending a garden. In our house in Pottsville, his plants grew along the driveway and in the back yard. There were also bushes, planted in front of the front porch, that grew red berries. My brother and I knew we could not eat the berries, but we loved squashing them and watching the red juice stain the sidewalk or our fingers.

If you climbed over the stone wall behind our back yard, you ended up in a farmer's orchard that had been allowed to grow wild. The wild blueberries we picked from there we often ate, although I don't remember ever washing them. That field was an enchanting place to play—we built forts and clubhouses,

Chapter Twenty-One

using the limbs that had fallen off of the trees. We went on adventures regularly, although I can't remember what they were all about. Nobody bothered us or warned us to be careful. As long as we came home when we were called, we were left alone. The group of kids I played with were mostly my brother's friends, four years younger than me, but I guess I found playing with them better than being alone, since none of my school friends lived on my block. Besides, I could boss them around, which I loved. Why they followed my commands I have no idea—maybe I was creative at coming up with new adventures?

The two things I remember with the most joy were my beautiful blue Columbia two-wheeled bicycle and my Flexible Flyer sled. For years I had scabs on my elbows and knees from falling off the bicycle. Since we lived on a steep hill, I had to walk my bike up the hill and ride it on Norwegian Street, which ran perpendicular to 22nd Street and at our end of town was fairly flat. I spent hours on that bicycle, and eventually I could ride the bike down the hill very fast when I came home. The hill was especially glorious when it snowed—perfect for riding a sled down to Market Street. I remember riding for so many hours that my cheeks, fingers, and toes tingled, and my nose ran like a faucet. Looking back with embarrassment, I think I wiped my runny nose on my sleeve. Again, the world was such a safe place that we rode our bikes or our sleds for hours without any grownups checking up on us.

Speaking of safe—my favorite story is about the milkman, the one who put things in the milk box. I loved his truck, with the sound of glass bottles rattling in their metal racks as he drove slowly around the neighborhood. It is hard to believe, but my parents let me ride around with the milkman as he made his rounds in our neighborhood. I loved helping him and listening to the rattling bottles. Can you imagine in today's world letting a young girl ride around with the milkman? I think he enjoyed my chatter and my company. He brought me safely home each time I rode with him. Hard to believe, but true.

Growing up Jewish in a small town in Pennsylvania was a very comfortable thing to do, certainly in the 1940's. Since all my close friends were Jewish too, I never felt different. My world outside of Yorkville Elementary School consisted of Day Camp or Hebrew School at the Jewish Community Center. My only brush with anti-Semitism during my childhood in Pottsville is an incident that had to do with the Brownies, the younger version of the Girl Scouts. There was a Brownie Troop at my elementary school. The girls who were Brownies got to wear their uniforms to school on meeting days, and I was thrilled when I got to be old enough to join. Besides the prestige of being a Brownie, I was particularly excited about getting to dress as one.

I got my uniform—a dress, a hat, and a Brownie pin—but sadly, I got to wear the regalia only once. Someone decided that Jewish girls couldn't join the Troop—I truly have no idea all these many years later whether it was the Brownies themselves or some authority in the Pottsville community who decided that we didn't fit in—but my time as a Brownie was very short-lived. I have the whole uniform in the childhood treasure box that lives in my closet. I still feel a sense of regret when I see that cute brown outfit, now ancient, nestled in tissue paper. It is interesting to note that up until that incident, even as the child of a Holocaust survivor, I had no idea that being Jewish might mean not fitting in.

In addition to taking part in sports of any kind from his days in Germany, my father loved Sunday drives into the Pennsylvania countryside. I can't remember my mother coming along for those rides—it was usually just my brother and me or me alone with him. Sometimes we just drove, and sometimes we went fishing in the streams that were still clear and pure in those days.

We talked as we drove, and I remember asking my father regularly, "Do you know where we are, Daddy?"

"No," he would reply, "but remember, all roads lead to Rome." I think that's where my love of traveling by car down unknown roads came from. I've always loved reading maps and navigating and have never felt scared of getting lost. Irwin, my late husband, called me "Christopher Columbus." Why not—my father taught me that all roads lead to Rome!

Considering what had gone on in his life in Germany in the

Chapter Twenty-One

1930s and '40s, my father never told me anything morose nor tragic about his parents or friends. I don't know if he was very resilient or if he was keeping it all inside, but he was cheerful and positive even after what I now know was a painful time for him. The only memory I have of how fragile he thought life was had to do with a recollection I have about our stamp collections. My parents got me a stamp book, too, but it was fairly empty, which caused me great embarrassment. I had several friends who had stamp books like mine, but their books were loaded with beautiful stamps that their parents could afford to buy them. Mine had only a measly offering of leftovers from my father's collection. One day, as we were looking at stamps on the third floor, I asked my father for some of his stamps for my book. He looked at me and said very calmly, "You can have them all when I'm dead." Shocked, I thought he was being selfish or that he was just being funny. Now, looking back at all the evidence, I think it is possible that he had a premonition that I would have his stamp collection before very long. It's not a very good memory for me.

Although I was too young to understand the toll the past twenty years had taken on my father, looking back I see that it clearly had affected his health, his thinking, and his view of the future. But he kept on smiling through it all.

Chapter Twenty-Two

Pottsville: The End

1954

By 1949, the sun had begun to set for the Arthur Meier family, but they didn't know it yet. My father had come out of the Army with a serious case of high blood pressure, untreatable in 1945. In addition, the hosiery business had really begun to go downhill. It is evident from his letters to his German friends that he was constantly searching for something else to do. His options were limited as he was burdened with a family to support—a wife, two children, and a house. By the 1950s, the decline of the coal industry was also affecting business in Pottsville. Not having enough money was surely the big issue affecting both my parents.

And then there was my mother's gall bladder. Yes, you read that correctly—I did say gall bladder. It's 1949 and my mother is spread out, writhing in pain, on the chaise lounge in my parents' bedroom. Apparently, she is having a gall bladder attack.

I have no idea how many of these attacks occurred before she ended up at Jefferson Hospital in Philadelphia having her gall bladder removed, but I remember them clearly even though they happened seventy years ago. My parents hired a Hungarian woman named Alexandria to live in and take care of my brother and me so my father could run the store while my mother was in the hospital. I was seven years old and in second grade, but my brother Jeffrey was only three and not in school yet. My parents must have found it hard to find live-in help because they hired this woman even though she spoke no English! None of us, of course, spoke Hungarian. Alexandria did such a poor job of taking care of us that my second grade teacher told me to bring my hairbrush to school. From then on until my mother got home, that lovely teacher brushed my hair every day when I got to school. My meticulous German father had a problem with Alexandria's lack of hygiene. In a letter to my mother in the hospital, he says that he gave me the job of talking to the

Chapter Twenty-Two

woman about bathing! In another letter he says that "Susan can take care of herself." It didn't make me feel good to read that. I was seven years old! So much for my childhood.

My mother saved all of my father's beautifully written letters to her, which she received while she was in the hospital, each begging her to have a positive attitude and get better. It appears that my father was alluding to a big problem that had nothing to do with her gall bladder. It seemed that my mother didn't want to come home—she wanted to stay with one of her sisters or her mother in Reading after she got out of the hospital. From my father's letters, it sounds as though he was dealing with someone who was having some sort of a nervous breakdown. Perhaps my mother had a premonition of things to come. Who knows? But it was in character for her—for the rest of her life she often displayed a fear that she was having a heart attack, often out of proportion to what was really wrong with her. I suspect these incidents were really panic attacks. What it was like for my father, having already lost so much in his short lifetime, comes through in his letters. Reading his letters is a glimpse of someone I don't remember—I have no memory of him ever being that emotional.

All of this stress was clearly not good for his heart condition. His doctor, Norman Wall, a family friend, was very concerned, but in 1950, the options for treatment were very limited. There was no blood pressure medicine nor open-heart surgery—none of the things at our disposal today. Finally, Norman Wall must have decided that he wanted my father to check into the hospital for a complete physical—or at least a 1953 version of one.

I still remember the Sunday we drove my father to the Good Samaritan Hospital, the Catholic Hospital where Jeffrey and I had been born. The hospital was staffed with nuns who were Nursing Sisters. I remember that day clearly—my father walking into the hospital, carrying his radio under one arm and the Sunday newspaper under the other.

Within a day or two, in the hospital, my father suffered at least one heart attack or perhaps two. He survived them, thanks to the Nursing Sisters who saved his life. How they did it years *before there was any form of a mechanical device to restart hearts is a mystery to me. The Sisters, some of whom were German, loved my father and the feeling was mutual. Perhaps they were customers of his at the store as well? In my box of childhood treasures, I have a small empty bottle of a German cologne called "4711 Kolnisch Wasser," from Cologne, Germany, that one of the nuns gave me while my father was in the hospital.*

Upon his release from the hospital in Pottsville in July 1953, my father was sent to the Veterans' Hospital in Lebanon, Pennsylvania. The protocol for patients who had had heart attacks was complete bed rest. It is shocking for me to type those words! It is tragic to contemplate that all the doctors could prescribe for my then 43-year-old father was complete bed rest! It was a death sentence.

Children were not allowed to visit patients in the VA hospital which meant that Jeffrey and I could only stand on the grass when we visited, looking up at my father waving to us from his hospital window. When I think back to this heartbreaking time, it seems as though it went on for far longer than four months in the summer of 1953.

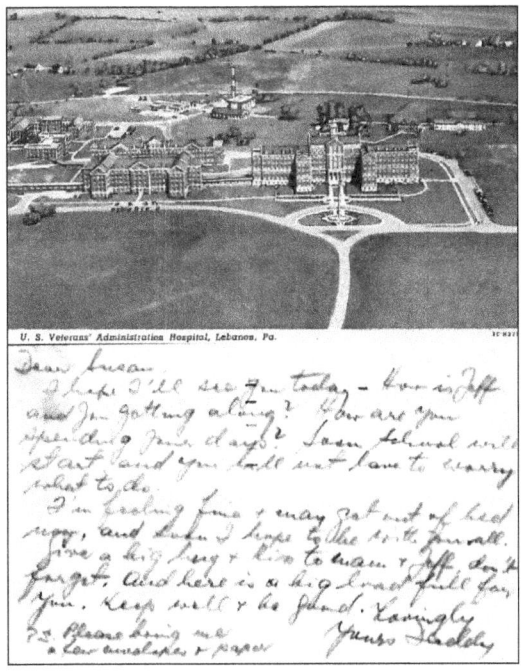

Chapter Twenty-Two

I have no memory of my father coming home, but apparently, he finally did in September.

Another thing I don't remember is at what point my parents decided to close down the store. The only clue I have is that the last thing my father bought for me on his last buying trip for the store was a set of three pins commemorating Queen Elizabeth's Coronation on June 2, 1953. I loved the pins—a crown, an orb, and a scepter. My mother got a job as a bookkeeper for the Jewish Community of Pottsville, and from then on, unknowingly, I held my breath as I watched my parents play out role reversals—he now playing the role of househusband while my mother went out to work each day.

Even as a child, I sensed just how frail my father's hold on life was. It felt as though we were walking on eggshells all of the time. He understood how sick he was and sometimes talked about it. Unfortunately, it was an accurate premonition. All it took was a young boy, dashing out in front of our car, unharmed, as my father picked my mother up from work and my brother and me up from Hebrew School late one afternoon, to shock him into his third and fatal heart attack less than an hour later. Arriving home, he dropped my mother and me off at the beginning of the driveway so we could go in the front door. Then he continued driving toward the garage with my brother Jeffrey sitting next to him. He drove into the garage, turned off the engine, and slumped over the steering wheel. My brother's screams brought us running through the house and out the back door.

I didn't realize that I had started to scream, too, until my mother told me to stop screaming. "He can hear you," she said, which, of course, was not true. My father had died instantly. Within minutes, the three of us heard the ambulance screech around the corner as it drove into our driveway. I still hate the sound of ambulances to this day. We watched the medics transfer my father's body from his car to the ambulance and drive away.

Unfortunately, in those days, children who lost a parent, particularly in the traumatic way that Jeffrey and I did, were not hauled off to a psychologist to work out their grief. It was still the Dark Ages when it came to dealing with the trauma children experience when losing a parent. I was told to "help your mother." And Jeffrey was thought too young to realize what was going on. I was allowed to go to the funeral, but he was not, a fact which still bothers him today.

I remember feeling tremendous guilt immediately after my father's death—he had asked me to go on one of our car rides the Sunday before he died, and I had refused to go. For a long time I carried the burden of that refusal with me. Guilt and a whole lot of magical thinking—I kept looking for him in groups of people, expecting to see him coming back, walking toward me. How could I have known as a child that what I was feeling were perfectly normal forms of grieving? Unfortunately, there was nobody to discuss this with, nor to tell me that such reactions were to be expected. Or to tell me that I would carry my unresolved grief with me forever.

My father's friends from Germany reacted with shock to the news of his death at such a young age. One letter was from Fritz—now called Fred—Valfer, one of the two other Jewish children in my father's elementary class in Gengenbach who was now living in New York. The two men had seen each other several times when my father went to New York on buying trips for the store. In this letter, Fritz tells my mother that his wife and daughter are in Europe and

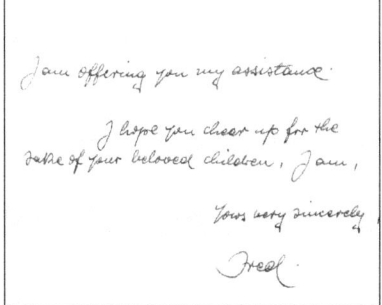

Chapter Twenty-Two

that she will tell the survivors from Gengenbach the news. His says that she will tell Mrs. Fetterer, his aunt, at whose house, "Arthur was like at home."

The second letter is from Franz Blum. He knew how sick my father was, and so his reaction is not shock, but sadness. His love for my father is obvious.

My Dear Sylvia :

I cannot tell you how disturbed I was when I got your letter. As your hand writing is so similar to Arthur's I did not realize until I had read the first page what happened. When I understood I could not continue to read, and my people in the office came to ask me what had happened when they saw me wiping away tears from my eyes.
I do not need to tell you, Dear Sylvia, how near I felt to Arthur whom I loved like a brother. All our childhood we have been together and now I am deeply unhappy having lost our good Arthur. Ulrica, my parents and all our family wish to express you our deepest sympathy and we only hope that you will be strong enough to bear the burden with which destiny charged you. We know what it means to lose a beloved husband who has been so good and tender: Arthur will certainly have told you that my sister lost her husband only half a year ago, with a ten years old boy.

Arthur's silence

In the meantime you certainly had my last week's letter and you may have seen that I was anxious to get news because/made me fear what so unhappily resulted. Knowing that Arthur had had two attacks within eight months I was ever so preoccupied because medical friends told me that a third attack would be fatal. –
Did Arthur enjoy at least the film of our old Gengenbach ?
Dear Sylvia, it is too hard and so upsetting that just the best ones and such young lives are going away. You may be sure that Arthur will be remembered by all of us and especially by myself as the best of friends, father and husband. Please explain to Susan and Jeffrey that far away from them there are good friends who are as unhappy as they are about the loss of their good Daddy.
I would like to know whether I can do anything for you. Please give me your new address as soon as you move to Reading.
I think that you ought to continue the claim Arthur started in Germany, and if you give me a copy of what he had done until now I shall indeed again with the lawyer in Offenburg and find out whether even additional claims – perhaps for a rent for the children – could be momentary presented.

Now, my Dear Sylvia, let us keep alive and continue our friendship and brotherly attachment, and if it is not much what I can express at least you may feel that I am very unhappy.

I remain with all good wishes hopes for you

very cordially yours

At the end of 1954, Helmut Breunig wrote to my family to offer us new year wishes for 1955, and also, interestingly enough, to make sure we were keeping our father in our thoughts!

The impact of my father's death was a burden I carried around with me my whole life. I was close to fifty years old before I thankfully found a wonderful psychologist who finally helped me see how that loss was still coloring decisions I was making forty years later.

Within months after my father died, my mother sold the house on 22nd Street and moved us to Reading—back home to her family. Sadly, my Coronation pins disappeared during the move, but I still think of them fondly.

My mother packed up all my father's treasures, including the letters and postcards from Germany and France, and they made it to Reading with us. Looking back over the years, I think the vision of that pile of letters was always tucked away in my

Chapter Twenty-Two

mind. Even though I didn't know what they said, I think I always believed that someday the letters would make it possible for me to read what my grandparents wrote about what they were experiencing.

Unfortunately, I see how the Holocaust, combined with my father's illness and death, helped to shape my view, by age eleven, of just how unsafe the world was and just how carefully I needed to keep control of life. I unconsciously believed that if I kept a really tight hold on what was going on, I could keep bad things from happening. What a big job that was going to be!

Chapter Twenty-Three

The Wise Family

While I never laid eyes on my father's parents, I never felt a shortage of relatives as I grew up. It took me years to understand that I didn't feel the void in my life because it was filled by my mother's huge family, headed by my immigrant Ukrainian grandparents, Anna and David Wise. David Wise escaped the Russian Army and came to North America in about 1903 with one of his two brothers. They couldn't get into the United States, so they went first to Canada. My grandfather's goal was to get to Reading, Pennsylvania where my grandmother, born Anna Rudolph, had family members who had already settled there. Eventually, he made it and then sent for his wife and baby son, Moshe Mechel—later to become one of my two Uncle Morrises—in 1905. And the family samovar—but that's another story.

It seems that the Rudolph family, already successful in business, did not lend much of a hand to their newly-arrived sister and her family. While my grandfather had learned the blacksmith trade in the Russian Army, I don't think he ever went to work for the Rudolphs in their scrap metal business. I wonder if perhaps they never invited him to? Instead, my grandparents ended up moving to a farm on the Pricetown Road outside Reading. Apparently, it seemed like the best way to feed and care for their rapidly growing family, eventually becoming seven children. What I know about "the farm" as it was referred to in the family is the stories my oldest aunts and uncles told me about how dreadful life was living on a farm—six days a week.

Since they were Orthodox Jews, they packed up all the children in their wagon, and pulled by their horse, traveled into Reading every Friday for "Shabbos," the Sabbath. My cousin Joyce told me that they stayed with "Tante Ruchel," whoever she was, until sundown on Saturday night. Then they all bundled back into the wagon and headed back to the farm and the hard-scrabble life of work waiting for them. I can't even imagine how difficult

Chapter Twenty-Three

it must have been. When my twin aunts said they raised their younger, by only a few years, brothers and sisters, they were not exaggerating! My mother, Sylvia, born on the farm on August 9, 1915, was the next to the last of the seven children.

The twins, Julia and Sarah, with their older brother Morris in between them on the farm

The three older Wise children at the one-room schoolhouse they attended in the country. Morris is standing by himself on the right in the second row and the twins are the second and third girls to his right in the second row

Farming turned out to be such a bad idea that eventually the family moved into the city of Reading, where they bought a four-story row house at 717 Moss Street. Even though the house in Reading had to have been an improvement over the farm, it must have been a very crowded place—for many years all seven children shared two bedrooms and all nine of them shared the outhouse. At some point in time, they finally added on to the back of the house, enlarged the kitchen on the first floor and built an indoor bathroom and one more bedroom upstairs. They added "back steps" which led from the kitchen to the new bedroom. But they left the "outhouse." I remember peeking into it as a child and shuddering at its crudeness. Hard to imagine nine people using it! Especially in the winter!

Like most early Pennsylvania row houses, the Wise house on Moss Street didn't have hallways—you walked through each room to get to the next one—and as was usually the tradition, there were three rooms on each floor. Years later I learned that they were called *Father, Son, and Holy Ghost* houses. On the first floor, you walked through the living room to get to the dining room and through the dining room to get to the kitchen.

On the second floor, in order to get to the bathroom—after it was added on—you had to go through two of the bedrooms! My grandparents lived in the house on Moss Street so long that I visited there often as a young child. I remember sleeping in the middle bedroom in a big, high metal bed and feeling my grandmother putting her hand on me in the bed as she felt her way to the bathroom at night. It is a lovely memory.

My grandfather acquired an old truck in which he collected and sold scraps of metal he found around Reading, perhaps to the Rudolph family, but I don't think he ever earned a decent living. My grandparents also collected old newspapers which they kept in the garage behind their house to sell for small amounts of money. As was common at that time, their large family meant that the older children left school and went to work at a very young age. The boys, Morris, Danny, and Roxy, all left school before they were in their teens and got jobs. Sarah and Julia, the twins, had to raise their younger siblings and help

Chapter Twenty-Three

do the housework. They both married quite young, which got them out of the house as soon as possible.

In 1933, my mother was the first member of her family to graduate from high school—Reading High School—the same school from which my brother and I graduated years later, me in 1960 and Jeffrey in 1965. It's interesting to note that a lack of education never stopped my uncles and aunts—a hunger for success won out as they made their way on the streets of America that were paved with gold, just as in the stories of many immigrant families.

All seven of the Wise children married, and my early childhood was spent seeing them, mostly in Reading, particularly for Jewish holidays. If I close my eyes, I can still remember the huge family, crowded around the dining room table in my grandparents' house on Moss Street for a Passover Seder or for a holiday dinner. We kids were relegated to a card table in the living room, but I always snuck into the dining room to share a chair with somebody. That is where I learned Yiddish—which they spoke so the children wouldn't understand them. That is how I learned many family secrets that my cousins never knew!

Sometimes I came from Pottsville to visit my grandparents at the same time my cousin Marlene, who lived in Lancaster, also came for a visit. Those visits were very special—my cousin was daring—and I got into trouble with her all of the time. Getting into trouble was rare for me—Marlene was always far braver than I was—and I loved that about her. Jumping up and down on the high beds upstairs and running up the front stairs through the bedrooms and down the back stairs over and over with my brother tagging along at the end as we ran drove the grownups crazy at family dinners and got us into trouble year after year, a memory that still makes me smile.

My grandfather was a quiet man, with a moustache that tickled when he kissed me. I don't remember ever having a conversation with him, but my mother loved him dearly, spoke well of him as a father, and grieved deeply when he died in 1950. A little-known family secret was that my grandfather had an earlier wife and two children who died in a Pogrom.

As a widower, he agreed to an arranged marriage with my grandmother before he left Ukraine. She told me that she always believed that he never loved her as much as he did his first wife. That may be, but clearly that did not interfere with their ability to produce progeny—she gave birth to five babies plus one set of twins, religiously, every two years, until they had seven children.

Ah, my grandmother! My grandmother, Anna Rudolph Wise, was a unique and very special lady. She taught herself to speak, read, and write English, using what we today call "invented spelling"—spelling by sounds. She kept a strictly kosher home, and if her family was going to a restaurant to eat, she would join them and nurse a cup of tea throughout dinner. She prayed three times a day, and for Shabbos, she lit tons of candles for various relatives, long-gone, some having died in Ukraine after she left. She even tore the toilet paper ahead of time and put it in a basket next to the toilet before the Sabbath. Her faith was incredibly deep—*she was the most authentically religious person I have ever known.*

Anna Wise was loved and respected by every one of her grandchildren. Each of us remembers having special conversations with her throughout our lives. I sat with her and talked for hours about her life near Kiev in Ukraine, about politics, and just about anything else I could think of. As a woman, she was born several generations too soon, but the success her children, grandchildren, and the following generations found was in large measure due to her influence—her love of learning, her intelligence, and her acceptance of each of us—foibles and all. She was a very smart lady who knew who she was and what she believed in. I don't believe she ever said or did anything in her entire life for effect—she was truly a genuinely completely honest soul.

The only flaw my grandmother had was one she carried with her from the Shtetl in Ukraine. When she watched the news on television and read the newspapers, which she did religiously, all the news was measured against her yardstick, "Is it good for the Jews?" Her view of everything that happened depended on the answer to that question. Sometimes, especially as I'm getting

Chapter Twenty-Three

older, I find myself asking the same question! Asking it always takes me by surprise.

My grandmother lived alone in that four-story house on Moss Street for 15 years after my grandfather died, until she was eighty years old! I spoke to her in her hospital room days before she died. *"I'm tired, Mein Kind (my child),"* she told me. *"My friends have all gone. I am ready."*

Her words made it a lot easier a few days later, early on the morning of Election Day in November 1964, to accept the news when the call came telling us that she had died. I had a big decision to make—it was the first time I was old enough to vote, but I sure didn't feel like doing it. And then I thought about what my grandmother would say if she knew I didn't vote—her admiration for the freedom she had acquired as an American compared to her life in Ukraine made her a true lover of democracy. Without hesitation, I got dressed and went to vote—for Lyndon Johnson—as I recall.

I still miss my grandmother even though she has been gone for 59 years. While growing up, I really never felt the void left by my shortage of grandparents thanks to her.

My twin aunts, Julia and Sarah also filled a large part of my life. I loved visiting them, too. Sarah and her husband Dave lived in Hazelton, a town in the coal region of Pennsylvania. They had a ladies' clothing store, so visits to them meant spending time looking at beautiful clothes. I also remember watching boxing matches on the tiny TV they had in the living room and reading the piles of Superman comics in my cousin Nathan's room. I made this sweet lady my son Adam's Godmother, although she didn't live long enough to see him grow up. Sarah died tragically young, alone, in August of 1972, in her early 60's.

Aunt Julia, the other twin, was a very special part of my life. She helped my father open *Hosiery Mills Outlet* by loaning him some money to help start the business until he bought out her share. She could always be counted on to babysit, and I spent a lot of time with her and her husband, Uncle Herman, in Reading.

I was a terrible eater as a child, so I remember memorable stand-offs between my Aunt Julia and me three times a day—breakfast, lunch, and dinner—whenever I stayed with her! To this day I can remember sitting in her kitchen with a healthy, but to me, enormous amount of completely inedible food, piled up high on the plate in front of me. She battled on, although, I don't think she ever won. The day my brother was born, we got the phone call from my father during lunch, in the middle of our usual mealtime battle. Believe it or not, when we hung up the phone, my Aunt Julia expected me to sit back down at the table and finish lunch!

Nobody ever worried about how I would occupy my time on those sometimes very long visits. There were no kids on the block, no children's toys in the house—both her children—my cousins Joyce and Bobby, were much older than I was and had gone off to college by the time I came for visits. I always thought of Joyce and Bobby as my older brother and sister, but they were not around to keep me company during those long stays with their parents. Bobby eventually married Kaye, who quickly became another older sister to me.

There was however, the "Third Floor," with its wall-to-wall closets with mirrored doors, filled with dresses, hats, shoes, and jewelry, all of which I spent hours trying on! I didn't even know there was such a thing as boredom—thankfully, it was a word I had never heard.

Both Joyce and Kaye made a big difference in my life as I got older. Kaye made sure I had, among other things, a sweet sixteen party and luggage for college. She listened to my complaints about my mother and never took sides. And Joyce took me along on car trips that always turned into adventures—like the time she took me to Lake Placid, New York where it turned out she had bought an old house to turn into a ski lodge. Joyce lived in an apartment on Rittenhouse Square in Philadelphia where I used to visit her. She was gone all day at law school or later, at her law office. I would take "Happy," a Welsh Corgi she had actually bought for me and my brother, but my mother wouldn't let us keep, and wander the streets of Philadelphia. Sometimes I stuffed newspaper in the front of her spike-heeled shoes and paraded around Rittenhouse Square. I was a tiny, young-looking

Chapter Twenty-Three

teenager and it is with horror that I contemplate what I looked like!

Aunt Julia and Uncle Herman bought me the only jewelry I owned as a child. The first gift was a monogrammed gold heart that Uncle Herman bought me at Tiffany's. Later, Aunt Julia added a gold charm bracelet and finally, a Jewish star with pearls in it on a gold chain to wear around my neck. Eventually, I put the star and the heart on the charm bracelet and when I look at it even now, I am reminded of their generosity to me.

The Wise Family – September 1947
My parents are sitting and standing on the left, with my mother holding my brother Jeffrey, and I am the smaller of the two girls, in the middle, with my cousin Marlene, between my grandparents

The night my father died on March 8, 1954, it was Julia and Herman who took Jeffrey, then six years old, and me, eleven, back to their house in Reading. My brother and I slept, huddled together, in one of the twin beds in the back bedroom, crying ourselves to sleep. My mother quickly moved us to Reading after school was done in June, thinking that her huge family would fill the void left by my father's death.

And fill the void they did—I spent the next ten years living in the *"sturm and drang"* that the large group of aunts, uncles, and cousins often created in each other's lives, and of course, in mine. *"The Girls"* were consistently pitted against *"The Boys"* in family feuds, with male chauvinism usually the winner. But the girls never gave in easily.

I always knew that I had to get away from the Wise family in order to grow up. When my first husband, Lawrie, my son, Adam, and I moved to Miami in 1971, a ghetto with palm trees that was 1200 miles away from Pennsylvania, I felt like I had finally escaped. While I give the family members credit for helping to shape me into the person I am today, I believe that I would never have fully become that person had I stayed in Reading. Fifty years later, I still feel like a bird let out of a cage.

I now know that the most important thing about getting away from Reading and the family is that this book has been written. I don't think I would ever have recognized the shortage that my missing grandparents—Sophie and Berthold Meier—left in my life if I had still been dwelling in the midst of that very deafening crowd—The Wise Family.

Chapter Twenty-Four

Meeting Helmut Breunig

August 1968

*L*awrie parked the rented Mercedes in front of the lake in Meersburg, just beyond the beautiful old pink castle we had just passed. Tired after the long ride from Gengenbach, the four of us climbed out of the car and stretched. As we did, I saw two men walking toward us. When they got close enough, I found myself staring at the younger man. He looked exactly the same as he did in the pictures all through my father's green photo album. It was Helmut Breunig, the man I'd waited my whole life to meet. An older man walked by his side. As they got closer, a thought began to nag at me. Just before they reached us, it hit me that the young man was NOT the man I'd come to see! The pictures in my father's album were thirty or even more years old. The man I'd come to see was now close to 60 years old. The gray-haired older man was the person I'd come to Germany to meet—my father's best friend.

Chapter Twenty-Four

When they reached us, the older man and I embraced. I was so overwhelmed I could barely speak. Finally, it occurred to me to introduce the Breunig men to my husband. Helmut, of course, knew Elfriede and Adolf Lohmüller from Gengenbach, and they warmly greeted each other.

Slowly, we began to walk to an apartment building across from the lake. We walked in and went up one flight of stairs. Helmut opened a door, and as we entered an apartment, his wife was waiting for us. She, too, was an older version of the woman in the pictures in the green photo album. Her English was quite good. We all chatted for a few minutes about my visit to Gengenbach. The small talk was making me feel impatient and disappointed—I'd been waiting years for this moment, and it seemed so stiff and formal and awkward. I didn't know how to explain to them how special this moment was to me. Meeting the man who was my father's best friend, the man who slept in the basement of my grandparents' house after my grandfather was sent to Dachau after Kristallnacht so my grandmother wouldn't be alone, was unbelievably special to me. Helmut invited us to sit down at the dining table that stood in the middle of the parlor of the apartment, a room filled with heavy dark furniture and lace curtains. Out came the wine glasses and the wine, a ritual I'd gotten used to after three days in Germany. Helmut made a toast welcoming us to his home, and we drank.

Then he stood up, walked over to a shelf in a buffet against the wall, and took something from it. He walked toward me, and when he reached where I was sitting, he moved behind me. As he put the object down on the table in front of me, he asked, "Do you know who this is?"

I looked down and saw a photograph of myself at about age three. It surprised me and I gasped, "That's me!" It really wasn't strange that he had my picture—he and my father wrote to each other regularly before my father's death, and, naturally, they must have exchanged pictures of their growing families. After all, there were several pictures of Helmut's son as a little boy in my father's album.

I could feel tears begin to well up in my eyes. And then, all of the feelings that had been collecting since I got to Gengenbach—happiness, sadness, discovery, loss, fear—flooded over me. I put my head down on my arms on the table and sobbed my heart out. When I eventually picked my head up and looked around, I saw that every person in the room was crying too.

Helmut Breunig had chosen to show me this picture because he understood how this would make me feel about his relationship with my father. He knew that I would realize what his keeping my picture all these years would mean to me. Even now, over fifty years later, I remember that moment and how his kind gesture reminded me of how much he loved my father. And what an enormous loss their parting in 1937 must have meant for these two men. My father's death left him grief-stricken and filled with pain. It still makes me cry when I think about that day in Meersburg, but I am so happy that I got to meet this very special man.

Chapter Twenty-Five

The Little Black Book

January 2000

The phone on my desk buzzed and I heard my secretary say, "Claudine Partouche's grandmother would like to meet you." I got up from my desk, opened my office door, and walked into the outer office.

An elegant woman dressed all in black was standing talking to my secretary. I put out my hand and said, "I'm Susan Moss Katz. It's so nice to meet you. Claudine is a darling little girl."

"I am Rosa Partouche," the woman said with a beautiful French accent. "I'm visiting from Paris, and I so wanted to meet the Director of this wonderful school my son and daughter-in-law have been telling me about. Claudine is so happy here, and she has learned so much English in such a short time!"

"Do you have time to come into my office and talk for a few minutes?" I asked.

"But of course," she replied. "My daughter-in-law will come for me when the school day is finished for Claudine."

Rosa Partouche followed me into my office and sat down in a chair in front of my desk. I sat next to her, and we began to talk. She told me how delighted she was that her granddaughter was a student in a Jewish Day School now that she was living in Miami. "You know," she said, "Many Jewish children in Paris attend Jewish schools. My son and daughter-in-law were so happy to find this school so close to their apartment when they moved to Miami." We discussed the difference between private and public schooling in America and in France for several minutes.

Then I asked Rosa where in Paris she lived, and when she told me, I shared with her that I had a cousin living in Paris, but that I had lost track of him after my father died. Much to my surprise the next thing that came out of my mouth was, "And my grandmother died in France during the Holocaust." I certainly hadn't planned to say that to this stranger I had met only minutes ago.

Chapter Twenty-Five

"Where?" she asked me with a look of surprise on her face. I told her that my grandmother, a Jew from Baden, Germany, had died of starvation at Camp de Gurs in southern France, close to the Spanish border on January 13, 1942.

"She is supposed to have a marked grave, but I am not sure that is true," I told her. "I would like to visit Gurs if her grave exists."

"You ought to call Serge Klarsfeld," she said. "He would know."

Now I certainly knew who Serge Klarsfeld was—a famous French Nazi-hunter, who, along with his wife Beate, had conducted the search for and the conviction of Klaus Barbie, the Butcher of Lyon, and many other French and German war criminals. But to call and ask him? "How would I do that?" I asked her in astonishment.

Reaching into her large black handbag, Rosa Partouche pulled out an old-fashioned little black leather address book, and as she thumbed through the pages, she said, "I'll give you his number in Paris."

Wordless, I quickly grabbed a pen and wrote down 'Serge Klarsfeld' and the phone number as she dictated it to me.

We spoke for a few more minutes and then her daughter-in-law and granddaughter appeared to take her home. We kissed goodbye, and they left. I stood and stared at the paper on which I had written the words 'Serge Klarsfeld' and the phone number. Then I picked up the phone and called my husband, Irwin. "You'll never guess what I'm holding in my hand," I said. And then I proceeded to tell him the story of what had just happened.

For two weeks I carried around and often stared at the piece of paper with the famous name and Paris phone number written on it. But I didn't do anything about it. I was seriously intimidated to be making this phone call. Even though I wanted desperately to speak with Serge Klarsfeld about my grandmother and Camp de Gurs, it felt to me like this busy important man surely had better things to do than speak with me. Finally, on a Sunday morning, summoning up enough determination to act, I locked myself in the den and dialed the number.

A man's voice answered, and in broken French I asked, "May I please speak with Serge Klarsfeld?"

In perfect English, he replied, "I am Serge Klarsfeld, Madame." My hand started shaking so badly that I could hardly hold the phone.

I told him how I had gotten his phone number from Rosa Partouche. Then I explained why I was calling—that I had always been told that there was an actual cemetery at Gurs and that my grandmother, who died of starvation in January of 1942, had had a Jewish funeral. I told him that I would like to go to Gurs to see her grave if there really was a possibility that it existed.

The cemetery at Gurs, he told me, really exists—in 1962 it had been leased to the Oberrat der Israeliten Baden, the High Council of the Israelites of Baden, for 99 years.

I will never forget his next words to me, "Go," he said. "If your grandmother died at Gurs, Madame, go! You will find her." If I close my eyes, I can still hear him saying it.

He went on to ask me about my grandfather, and I told him that I knew my grandfather had survived Gurs and eventually was put on a train which went to Drancy, outside of Paris. I told him that I was told that my grandfather was finally sent to Bergen Belsen on Transport 50 where he died. "No, Madame," he said. "If your grandfather was on Transport 50, he was sent to Maidanek, and if he survived the journey, he went on to Sobibor where he would have been gassed upon his arrival. He said all of this so fluently that he sounded like a computer spitting out facts.

Again, he encouraged me to go to Gurs and suggested I call him again if he could be of further help. And then we said goodbye. I sat staring at the phone in my hand for heaven knows how long. Then I got up and ran out of the den, screaming, "Irwin!" as I tore down the steps.

Chapter Twenty-Six
Serge Klarsfeld: French Nazi-Hunter

Serge Klarsfeld is a Romanian-born French activist and Nazi hunter known for documenting the Holocaust in order to establish a record of what occurred and to enable the capture and prosecution of war criminals. He was born in Bucharest into a family of Romanian Jews. They migrated to France before the Second World War began. In 1943, his father was arrested by the SS in Nice during a round-up ordered by Alois Brunner. Deported to the Auschwitz Concentration Camp, Klarsfeld's father died there. His mother and sister survived the war in Vichy France, helped by the underground French Resistance beginning in late 1943. Young Serge was cared for in a home for Jewish children operated by the OSE (Oeuvre de Secours aux Enfants) organization.

Serge married Beate Künzel in 1963 and settled in Paris. Their son, Arno Klarsfeld was born in 1965, became a human rights attorney, and worked for Nicolas Sarkozy while he was Minister of the Interior.

Serge and Beate Klarsfeld are most famous for their contribution to the eventual conviction for war crimes of the infamous *Nikolaus (Klaus) Barbie*, who was an SS and Gestapo functionary during the Nazi era. After the German conquest and occupation of the Netherlands, Barbie was assigned to Amsterdam. In 1942 he was sent to Dijon, France, in the Occupied Zone. In November of the same year, at the age of 29, he was assigned to Lyon as the head of the local Gestapo. He established his headquarters at the Hôtel Terminus in Lyon, where he personally tortured adult and child prisoners, breaking extremities, using electroshock and sexually abusing

Chapter Twenty-Six

them (including with dogs), among other methods. He was known as the *"Butcher of Lyon"* for having personally tortured French prisoners of the Gestapo while stationed in Lyon, France. In April 1944, Barbie ordered the deportation to Auschwitz of a group of 44 Jewish children from an orphanage at Izieu.

Historians estimate that Barbie was directly responsible for the deaths of up to 14,000 people. He arrested Jean Moulin, one of the highest-ranking members of the French Resistance and his most prominent captive. In 1943, he was awarded the Iron Cross First Class by Adolf Hitler for his campaign against the French Resistance and the capture of Moulin.

After the war, United States intelligence services employed him for their anti-Marxist efforts and also helped him escape to Bolivia, in South America.

The West German Intelligence Service later recruited him. Barbie was suspected of having had a hand in the Bolivian Coup d'État orchestrated by Luis García Meza Tejada in 1980. After the fall of the dictatorship, Barbie no longer had the protection of the government in La Paz, and in 1983, and with the help of Serge Klarsfeld, was finally extradited to France, where he was convicted of crimes against humanity four years later. Claus Barbie died of cancer in prison on September 25, 1991.

Serge Klarsfeld is considered the world's leading authority on the horrors inflicted on French Jews by the Nazis. The good he has done in the world includes the miraculous gift he gave me of finding my grandmother.

Chapter Twenty-Seven

Go! You Will Find Her!

July 16, 2000

*F*rom the moment I went tearing down the steps yelling about my conversation with Serge Klarsfeld, Irwin began planning our trip to France. He seemed to have no doubt about whether or not we would find Sophie Meier's grave. Today, a simple Google inquiry as to the names of those buried in the cemetery at Gurs would have given us the answer we needed. But back in 2000, my quest to find the grave of my grandmother was still best done by airplane and car, with the help of my very curious and tenacious husband.

Irwin discovered that the only way to get to Pau, France, the nearest city to Camp de Gurs, was by car from Toulouse, France. And the best way to get to Toulouse was from Gatwick Airport in England. Unfortunately, there were no flights from Miami to Gatwick, only to Heathrow Airport. So, it turned out that we would have to fly from Miami to Heathrow, take a bus from Heathrow to Gatwick, fly from Gatwick to Toulouse, where we would rent a car and drive to Pau. If we were doing the trip today, we could fly from Miami to Paris and from Paris to Pau. But, in 2000, it was a lot harder. Undaunted, Irwin planned and got us ticketed for July 16, 2000. Next, he set about finding a hotel for us to stay in for two nights in Pau. Finally, he worked on finding the route to drive from Pau to Camp de Gurs. No MapQuest in 2000—Triple A was the go-to-place for maps in those days. It turned out that we had to drive southwest from Pau for just under an hour to the town of Oloron-Sainte-Marie, in Basque country. Gurs was beyond there, in the direction of the Pyrenees.

While Irwin was obsessed with planning our trip, I was obsessed over what I would do if we were successful at finding Sophie Roland Meier's grave. What would I take with me that would be meaningful?

Chapter Twenty-Seven

And now, finally, here it is—July 16th—and we are sitting on the plane at Miami Airport, waiting for takeoff. It feels just like any other vacation trip. Until I think about where I'm going and what I finally decided to take with me that is now packed in my luggage:

- *A gold and diamond ring which meant so much to the lady whose grave I'm hoping to find that she baked it in a cookie and mailed it to her son in America after Kristallnacht...the only thing the Nazis didn't get.*
- *A beautiful, faded photograph from the green photo album, taken about 1915, of a mother and a son—my grandmother with my father when he was a young boy.*
- *A picture postcard of Gengenbach, also from the green photo album.*
- *From my own photo album, a much newer picture of a father and his daughter taken about 1944—it is a picture of my father and me taken in a park in Columbia, South Carolina when we went to visit him while he was in the Army.*
- *Three sixty-year-old, sad postcards going back where they came from...going back to Gurs where Sophie wrote them in 1941—it seems only fitting that the postcards travel back to visit the lady who wrote them. It is too late to give her what she desperately asked for—soap and a way out of the dreadful place she found herself in.*
- *A Reform Jewish prayer book containing the Kaddish memorial prayer and poems to read for the dead and a Yahrzeit candle, the kind Jews light to mark the memorial of someone's death. Finally, 58 years after her death and burial, someone from Sophie's family will again say Kaddish at her grave.*
- *A stone to leave on the grave.*

Anyone looking in my luggage would see that this trip was clearly not your average vacation trip to the French countryside. But it is luggage that was packed by an optimist.

When we finally arrived at Gatwick Airport, we got on the short flight to Toulouse. Then Irwin and I picked up the rental car, and, following the maps, drove to Pau, a small French city, and arrived at the hotel in the center of the city where we checked in. They were kind enough to make us some eggs, so we at least had some food in our stomachs before we fell into the bed, exhausted from the 36-hour trip from Miami. Irwin fell right to sleep, but I only dozed off and on. The fear of what I would—or would not find—tortured me until morning finally came.

Chapter Twenty-Eight

Camp de Gurs

July 18-19, 2000

After breakfast at the hotel in Pau, armed with the maps that showed us the route, we headed for Gurs. I was feeling very excited but nervous traveling to this place I thought of as hell.

Oloron-Sainte-Marie, the place where the trains with the Jews from Baden had arrived, turned out to be a smallish pretty town, but our map showed that we needed to go through the town and continue into the countryside. The farmhouses gradually became farther and farther apart, and the fields grew bigger and bigger.

There had been no guidebooks by "The Lonely Planet" or "Fodor's" describing the route to Camp de Gurs—no descriptions of what we'd see along the way. We had no idea what to expect as we drove what was supposed to be a distance of 13 km. We could see by the map that we were driving in the right direction, but nothing appeared to tell us that we were actually going to locate what we had come all these thousands of miles to find.

And then finally, in the distance, we spotted a large white billboard on the left-hand side of the country road. My high school French was still passable enough to read and understand what it said. The sign said that this was the internment camp in which German Jews were housed during World War II—Camp de Gurs. Reading the billboard, I began to cry—we had found the camp. Now I wondered what else we would find.

Chapter Twenty-Eight

We looked around and saw nothing else but fields. Puzzled, we drove on a little farther, expecting to come upon a cemetery, but all we saw were more fields and little buildings. Finally, down the road on the left, we spied a farmhouse.

Excited to see a sign of humanity, we stopped, thinking we could ask for directions. While Irwin waited in the car, I climbed the farmhouse steps and knocked on the door. A woman came to the door, and, in my rusty French, I tried to explain what we were looking for. The woman managed, in French and very broken English, to indicate that we had found the right place and that we should wait—her husband would be coming home soon, and he would show us the cemetery. I went back to the car and told Irwin what she said. Then we waited.

Sure enough, about ten minutes later, a car came down the road and pulled into the driveway. The woman's husband, a French farmer, spoke passable English. He led us down a dirt road just past the farmhouse, explaining what we were seeing.

The farmer showed us some stumps of wood sticking out of the ground that were all that was left of the foundation of one of the camp's original barracks: Ilôt A to H housed the men, while Ilôt I to M housed the women. From their letters, I knew that Berthold was in Ilôt E and Sophie in Ilôt I.

Camp de Gurs in 1940 when Sophie and Berthold Meier were imprisoned there

A drawing of Ilôt H at Gurs

Finally, we came to a grassy track which led to something in the distance. The farmer pointed down the track and told us to walk that way—there we would find what we are looking for—the cemetery.

Irwin and I begin to slowly follow the track. I could feel my stomach turn over and a wave of nausea come over me. What if I came all this way after so many years of praying for this very day—only to fail? What if my grandmother's grave was not here? What if it was? I felt like my heart had stopped, too overcome with anxiety to keep beating. I must have looked ghastly because Irwin reached over and took my hand.

Finally, in the distance, we saw a wrought iron fence with a double gate.

Chapter Twenty-Eight

As we got closer, we could see rows and rows of white tombstones, all alike, stretching into the distance. Behind that was a farmer's field and, in the distance, beyond that, we could see the green foothills of the Pyrenees. Irwin pushed open the gate, and we walked in. Within seconds, we were looking at each other in confusion. All of the names were Spanish! We knew that this cemetery was originally used to bury refugees who died escaping from the Spanish Civil War. They were imprisoned here by the French when they were caught crossing the border from Spain. These were the first people to occupy the barracks that were later occupied by the Jews of Baden. But where were the Jews?

We kept walking on a path down the middle of the cemetery with rows of graves on either side, and, at last, we were excited to see a tombstone with a German name, a German town, and a date of 1942 under it. We looked at each other with relief.

Irwin said, "I'll take the right side and you take the left." We began walking up and down rows of graves. We each came across several "Meier" and "Meyer" and "Maier" graves, but no "Sophie Meier." None of the towns said "Gengenbach," either. I had walked down two or three rows when I heard Irwin call out my name. I looked up to see him standing a few rows ahead of me on the other side of the path. Had he found my grandmother? Was it really possible?

I stopped, overcome with conflict as my heart began to pound, and then I finally began to walk slowly toward where Irwin was standing. I felt tremendous dread with each step.

| 156 |

When I got to the grave he was standing in front of, I looked down and read the words on the tombstone: Sophie Meier, 1878–1942, Gengenbach.

I dropped to my knees and began to sob. I had found her.

Irwin kept his promise to leave me alone at my grandmother's grave, and he walked off into the cemetery. Carefully, weeping as I did it, I unpacked the postcards and the faded photographs. Then I took out the gold and diamond ring and the stone I had brought and placed them on top of my grandmother's tombstone.

My father had never gotten to say Kaddish at his mother's grave, so I said it for him, in his place. If he had been alive at this very moment, he would have been six days away from his 90th birthday. If he had lived. But he didn't. I sobbed as I recited the Mourner's Kaddish and a poem I had chosen. Then I lit the Yahrzeit candle, put it down, and sat down in front of the grave.

The birds were singing as I sat in the shadow of two maple trees at the grave marked with the words: Sophie Meier, 1878—1942, Gengenbach. The birds and the leaves made beautiful music. It was a lovely setting, a grassy slope of a hill overlooking the Pyrenees. Far lovelier than I could have imagined. The peaceful, lovely cemetery stands in stark contrast to the way things were in Camp de Gurs in 1942 when Sophie Meier starved to death. The lady whose beautifully monogrammed tablecloths and napkins survive to this day, carried by her son in his trunk to America, had died of starvation in this desolate place, wishing only for a coat, food, and soap.

Chapter Twenty-Eight

Sixty Women on Sixty Pallets

By Sylvia Cohn
1941
Camp de Gurs, France

Sixty women on sixty pallets of hard straw
Wind howling round the barracks, cold and raw
And we cannot tell the day from night
Because both the doors are shut tight
This cursed damp around us wraps
Its icy fingers through a thousand cracks
Penetrating through blanket, coat and dress
Chilled to the bone to our distress
On sixty pallets sixty women are trying
To stifle the muffled sounds of their crying
Shivering, cold and fearful, hoping for a better tomorrow
As they press their hands to their mouths in sorrow.

The poem by Sylvia Cohn describes the "hoping for a better tomorrow" that Sophie Meier never got. But my God, what peace Sophie lies in compared to her husband, my poor grandfather

Berthold. Heaven only knows where or how he died or where his bones or ashes ended up resting. I found her grave, but I knew I would never find his. His remains at Maidanek or Sobibor, or wherever they ended up, were not something I could ever find.

I never knew how much I needed to find this grave. I think I had never wanted anything more. Strangely enough, for the first time in my life, I felt a sense of peace and fulfillment. I talked to my grandmother and told her about the green photo album and how I still treasured it. I showed her the pictures of her with my father and the one of my father and me. Weeping, I told her that her beautiful son had lived only twelve years after she died. I explained to her that I now owned her beautiful gold ring, her silver pieces and monogrammed linens, that I was named after her and so all those beautiful objects that said SR were mine now.

All these things that up until that moment had just produced a sense of melancholy in me—no sense of who they really belonged to—who had created the beautiful SR monogram on them and really used them in daily life suddenly brought me a sense of peace. Now I knew. I was finally sitting in front of her grave.

After several hours, Irwin came back. And what, you might ask me, was he doing while I was at my grandmother's grave? My very special, very dear husband told me that he had spent his time at the cemetery walking up and down each and every row of graves, reciting the name on every tombstone out loud. He said he did it because he knew that many of these graves would never have a visitor. I smiled at him, feeling very lucky to have such a special person with whom to share this incredible experience.

Sitting together with Irwin at Sophie's tombstone, I began to think about the fact that today and tomorrow were probably going to be my one and only visit to this cemetery. I began to wish I had a way of memorializing my visit, and after a while, an idea began to form in my head. I turned to Irwin and said, "I have an idea. When we get back to Pau, let's look for an art store so I can get paper and chalks to do a grave rubbing of the tombstone tomorrow."

Irwin's face lit up, and he agreed with me immediately. I packed up my belongings, leaving the Yahrzeit candle burning in

Chapter Twenty-Eight

front of Sophie's grave. We slowly walked back to the car and headed back to Pau. My feeling of satisfaction stayed with me as we drove, and although I was exhausted, I looked forward eagerly to going back to Gurs the next day.

~

Wednesday, July 19, 2000

We arrived the second day at the cemetery with some new supplies. Irwin carried a pot of bright red flowers, and I carried the things I had bought in the art store in Pau. Today I was here for a different reason. Today I came for myself. To say Kaddish for the lady who was my grandmother. Whose name is mine now. Whose ring is mine now. Whose postcards and pictures are mine now, too. Whose linens monogrammed with SR and silver serving pieces are mine now.

Irwin went off and left me alone again. I said Kaddish and then I sat down in the grass and had another long conversation with the lady whose grave was in front of me. I wept quietly as I did all of this. It made me feel sad to think that this was the one grave I wasn't going to ever see again. After a time, Irwin came back.

Together we did the grave rubbing and then we rolled the sheet of paper up carefully and placed it in the cardboard tube we had bought. I put the flowers down in front of the gravestone. This grave had a visitor. It took 58 years, but somebody finally came. I felt as though my grandmother had finally become believable to me. She really existed!

Leaving was incredibly hard for me to do. As I walked away for the last time, I snapped pictures of the grave, the red flowers growing smaller and smaller. Finding my grandmother's grave and knowing that it existed would have to be enough for me.

I knew that I was no longer the same person who had traveled to Camp de Gurs. The biggest change in me was that now I wanted to learn more about my grandparents, Sophie and Berthold Meier. Now I felt a moral obligation to find out what happened to them so they would not be forgotten.

After 60 years, the Queen of Fear had finally left the Cave of Avoidance.

Chapter Twenty-Nine

A Visa Too Late

January 6, 1943

The idea that Emma Lazarus referred to on the Statue of Liberty that America is a haven for "huddled masses yearning to breathe free" is and always has been an idealization. The reality is that the American immigration policy has always been affected by prejudice and economic pressures which have influenced public opinion and legislation right up until today. "I think Americans have a very hard time deciding what kind of a country they want to have..." are the words of Peter Hayes, an American Holocaust scholar, expressed at the beginning of Ken Burns' series The U.S. and the Holocaust, *shown on PBS in 2022. How true!!!*

The immigration statistics for the years of the Holocaust clearly reflect the pressures and prejudices against Jews. The increasingly desperate situation of Jews in Germany, Austria, Czechoslovakia, Hungary, Poland, and other countries in Europe, all wanting to come to America, was affected by American immigration policies. Between 1933 and 1945, the quota of 27,370 German immigrants allowed per year was never met. Franklin Roosevelt wanted to do more for immigrants than he was able to do. His hands were tied by the anti-immigrant sentiment which pervaded large parts of the U.S. population and government. Consistent with overall anti-immigrant sentiments among government officials and in the country, the State Department viewed quotas as limits, rather than goals, and did not try to meet the quotas. Between 1933 and 1941, for example, roughly 118,000 German quota slots that could have been used went unfilled.

By 1938, there were more applications for visas on file than there were Jews left in Germany. At the end of 1939, the State Department had received 309,000 applications from applicants having Non-Quota Immigration status. However, no matter

Chapter Twenty-Nine

how many applications were received, few visas were issued by the U.S. State Department, which condemned most rejected applicants to death. Many Jews failed in their attempt to find freedom, among them 20,000 Jewish children who died because they were refused visas to come to the United States.

While the United States did accept 225,000 refugees, more than any other sovereign country during the Holocaust, of the 9,000,000 Jews in Europe in 1933, two out of every three were dead by the end of the Nazi nightmare. Among them were Sophie and Berthold Meier, my grandparents, and many other members of my family.

The policy of the Visa Division of the State Department, presided over by Breckinridge Long, the former ambassador to Italy, from 1940 to 1944, was dreadful. This meant that obtaining a visa was virtually impossible. During his time in the State Department, Long placed security concerns well over humanitarian concerns, because he and his subordinates were really driven by anti-Semitism, xenophobia, and a fear of spies and socialists who might infiltrate the U.S. as European immigrants.

They put into place stricter rules governing proof of support, called "affidavits," which meant that applicants now needed two financial affidavits instead of one to apply for a visa, which went a long way toward supporting Breckinridge Long's priorities. In July 1941 the State Department announced the new policy called the "Relatives Rule," in which all visa applications needed to be reviewed in Washington, D.C. by an inter-department visa review committee comprised of State, Justice, Intelligence, Military, and FBI Department representatives. Needless to say, this bureaucracy severely lengthened the process of obtaining a visa to the U.S. and successfully met the goal set by this odious man.

When the Nazis began their concerted effort to rid Europe of all its Jews, the Atlantic Ocean stood between the people trying to get out of Europe and into the Americas, both North and South. The difficulties of obtaining a paid ticket made passage on a ship an important part of the immigration attempt. You couldn't just walk for days and get to a border. Some Jews were lucky—they bought and paid for their visas and passages and made it safely to the other shore. Sometimes that didn't work out—the most famous example of this is the "Saint Louis," the ship that left Hamburg, Germany on May 13, 1939 and got turned away from Cuba, the United States, and Canada. The ship had to head back to Europe, where some of its passengers went to their eventual deaths. I had a friend, the late Hilda Gernsheimer, whose mother, father, and sister were on that ill-fated ship and who perished at the hands of the Nazis upon their return to Europe.

From the moment he got to America in 1937, my father started working on getting visas for his parents. In October 1940, when all the Jews of Baden were sent to Camp de Gurs in France, his urgency to do so increased tremendously. This is the first letter my father got from his parents after they arrived at Gurs.

Berthold Meier
Stat. Oloron-Sainte-Marie
29.10.1940

Dear Arthur,
Since Your last letter from the 8. 10. which we received on the 21. 10, the quite several has occurred for us. On Tuesday evening we had to leave with a term of only 1 hour our nice native country for good and might take only the most necessary hand luggage as well as per person 100 Mk. We landed after a journey of 60 hours in the above address where we must remain after our supposition probably longer time. Mummy lies 10 minutes of me in another camp where also aunt of Lahr, the Kippenheimer with the 97-year-old aunt and Elise of Pforzheim lie. Just I wanted to bring Mummy her suitcase, however, I did not see her, but Aunt Sophie

We lie about 10 km of the Spanish border. I do not want to

| 165 |

Chapter Twenty-Nine

describe our situation to you and make you sorrowfully, we stand here as beggars, it is the only reassurance for us that we have saved at least our life. Possibly it is to our luck to come rather abroad. Do your most possible if it is in the time. Something more exact I cannot write to you for the time, as soon as possible I write more. Only the community holds us straight, otherwise many would commit suicide. I write in the standing position, you will be able to read it, however. Soon give me answer and would be warmly greeted from your father. – The personal treatment by the French officers and camp officials is good. Write Fritz that all Gengenbacher are here.

Yesterday dear Arthur, some circumstances were explained: If you are married and American citizen, you can request for us. Get in contact with our guarantor whether he wants to renew the guarantee for us. There is no other rescue for us. The nights are very cold, we lie 1000 Meter high and at night we freeze very much. If you undertake something, only the American Consulate in France is possible. Undertake what stands in your power and save us from this misery.

Again hearty greetings, Your father

(Other handwriting): Please write the address from Fritz, I do not know if the old Address still is ok. Greetings Adolf Valfer

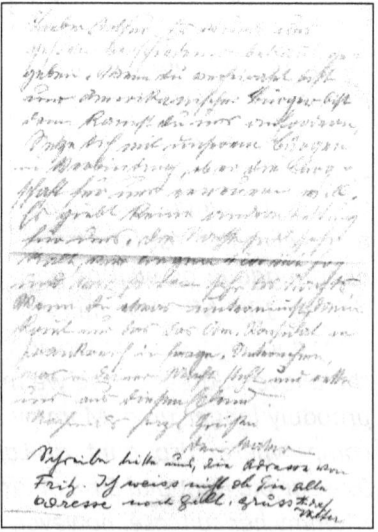

A Visa Too Late

The main topic of most of the letters that my grandparents wrote from Gurs continued to be about getting passage to America. It was clear that my grandparents didn't understand how desperately my father was trying, but failing, to get them out.

After his mother, Sophie, starved to death and was buried at Gurs in January 1942, my father became frantic at trying to get his father, Berthold, out of France. My father engaged in extensive communication with the U.S. State Department and also with HIAS, the Hebrew Immigrant Aid and Sheltering Society. I found many of these letters among the paperwork my mother had saved. Meanwhile, his father was being moved from camp to camp in France—from Gurs to Récébédou to Nexon.

Among the piles of paperwork, I found a positive piece of correspondence that did not need translating—a telegram dated October 23, 1942 from HIAS, telling my father that the State Department had finally granted advisory approval of his application for a visa for his father.

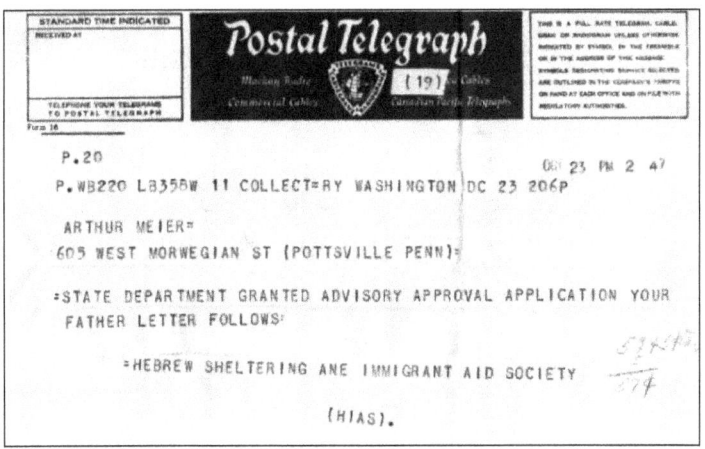

A letter dated December 3, 1942, from the State Department, requesting reimbursement of $3.72 for a telegram sent to Marseille said that the visa for Berthold Meier had been sent to the authorities in Marseille. These communications were puzzling to me at first as I knew my grandfather had not gotten to America! It took until long after I began my work with Martin Ruch and his translating the last letter that I came to understand

Chapter Twenty-Nine

just how close to successful my father's attempts to get his father out of France actually were! It was one of the most painful surprises I encountered during my years of research.

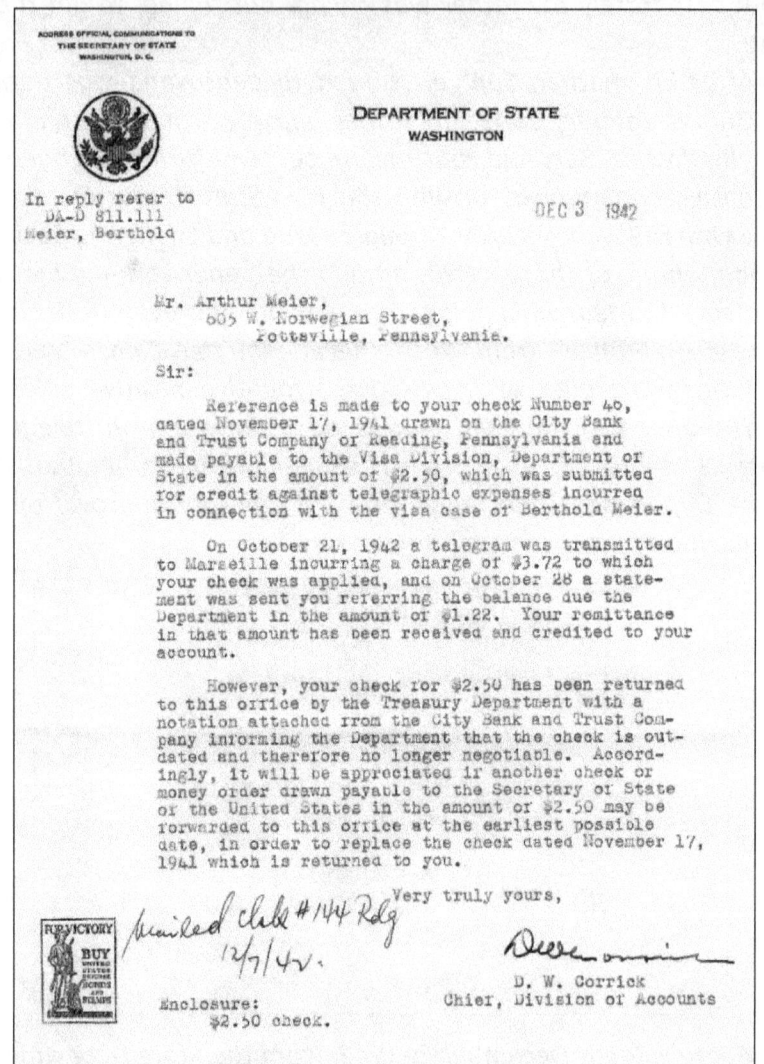

Choosing which letter to send to Martin to translate was random since I couldn't read them, so I went by the dates—trying to send them in the chronological order in which they were written. One letter kept getting pushed to the back of the line. It was written in German, dated January 1943, later than many of the others, and was addressed to someone named Sally Isaac, a name that meant nothing to me. When I finally took a good look at the letter, I discovered, much to my surprise, that the writer was my father, himself! The letter, sent to Diessenhofen, Switzerland, had come back marked "Return to Sender" and "No Service Available," and my father had kept it.

When I finally sent that letter to Martin to translate, I had no idea of its incredible significance to the story I am telling. In addition to being one of the few pieces of mail I have that my father actually wrote in German, the translation gave me a startling glimpse into just how frustratingly personal to the Meier family the immigration experience was during the Holocaust. Before reading the translation, I knew nothing about the tragedy that prevented my grandfather's safe passage out of France.

Here's what was in the letter that my father wrote to Sally and Berta Isaac. The new family member my father is referring to is, of course, me.

Pottsville, PA Jan. 6, 1942
(It was actually 1943—6 days into the new year)

My Dear Ones,
   Laws in this country forbid correspondence with enemy countries or countries occupied by enemies. Vichy France has been included since Hitler's occupation. This ended my connection with my dear father in Camp de Nexon near Limoges, an end that came so surprisingly quickly that the emigration that had just been in the way was cancelled. The State Dept. in Washington had issued an immigration permit and had already instructed the Consul in Marseilles to give a visa. I had paid $520 to HIAS for the ship's card and telegraphed my father. This alone happened about 10 days before the occupation and I don't know if my father got to know about it, and if he even knows that he was about to emigrate, because I haven't heard from him since. I will try to communicate with him through the Red Cross. If he were in Switzerland, Spain or Portugal, everything could continue and he could get an American visa, because everyone still does everything to save these poor creatures from death.

Chapter Twenty-Nine

> *On December 24th we got a new family member. So Papa became Grandpa without being able to participate in this joy. He doesn't know, of course. A beautiful daughter. Mom and daughter are both fine. Susan Rita is her name (named after Mama blessed Sophie Roland). She gives us much joy, and everyone who sees her says she is a reflection of my mother.*
>
> *We don't live in Reading anymore. Our new address is A.M. 605 W. Norwegian St., Pottsville. How are you yourselves? Where is Hella and family? Hopefully you are all safe and sound in a place where salvation and redemption can be seen freely and confidently. My wife, Susan and I send our best wishes and greetings.*
> *Your, Arthur*

I had listened sadly to all the tragic stories of immigration and visas and boats all my life without relating to them personally until Martin translated the "Sally Isaac" letter. In that letter, I discovered just how close my grandfather Berthold had come to getting safely into the United States before he was killed by the Nazis. I found myself wishing that this important letter had been translated while my mother was still living so I could have asked her how my father dealt with the tragedy my father spoke of in this letter to Sally Isaacs. His shocking letter to the Isaacs shows that my father knew that just before Berthold Meier's visa came through, the Germans had taken over Vichy France in August 1942, but not what eventually happened to his father.

Because my father did not know the truth of what had happened to his father, he did not give up. He went on searching for his father anywhere he could find help. Now in the Army, my father was also corresponding with a group called "Selfhelp of Emigres from Central Europe, Inc.", which merged in July of 1943 with the National Council of Jewish Women. In October of 1944, my father was still writing letters to these groups and to the Red Cross trying to locate his now missing father under the "Refugees Relative Registration." In them, he tells them that my grandfather was not sent to Drancy from Récébédou where the last letter I have was written, but rather from Camp de Nexon

A Visa Too Late

in Haut Vienne, France. My grandfather may even have been moved one more time as the place of departure to Drancy is listed as Noé, not Nexon.

One of the most tragic letters in my collection of tragic letters is the last one I found, dated April 17, 1945, in which HIAS notifies my father that nothing further can be done until his father is located. Berthold Meier was already dead two years, his death tragically unknown to his son, who was still frantically trying to find him.

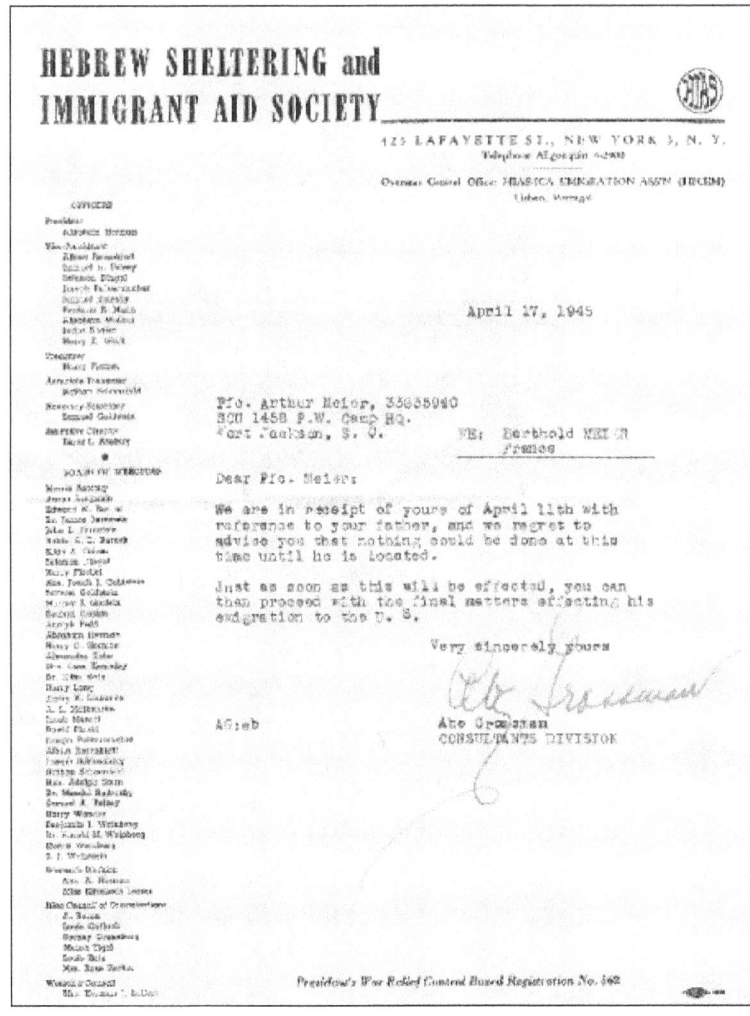

Chapter Twenty-Nine

I have no idea how or when my father actually got word of his father's death. However, even then, he got the wrong information! I found this document among his papers, written in his handwriting. The date of his father's death was wrong—his father was still very much alive on December 31, 1942. In addition, my family also believed that Berthold Meier died at Bergen Belsen until the year 2000 when Serge Klarsfeld told me the truth!

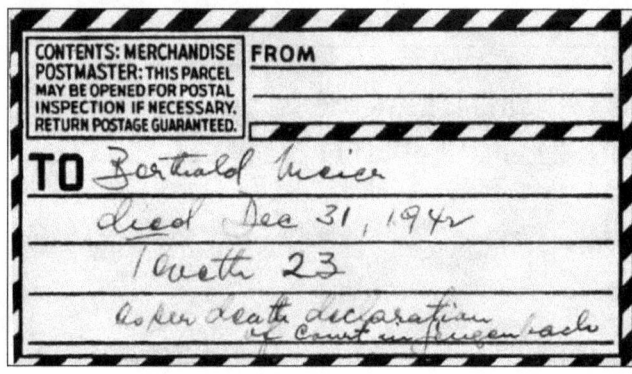

I understand now that my father never knew how his father's tragic story really ended. The facts are that after the takeover of France by the Germans, the 3,907 Jews who were still alive in the detention camps in the south of France, including my grandfather, were sent systematically, by train, to the camp at Drancy near Paris.

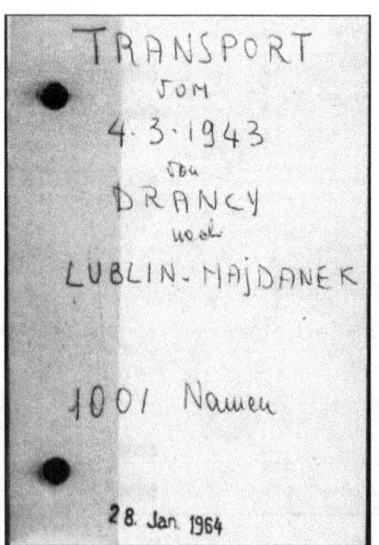

My grandfather was sent from Camp de Nexon or Noé to Drancy on February 26, 1943. Those Jews who lived through the trip to Drancy were then sent east to German extermination camps. Most of the Jews ended up at Auschwitz-Birkenau, including my grandfather's sister Elise Meier Daube.

A Visa Too Late

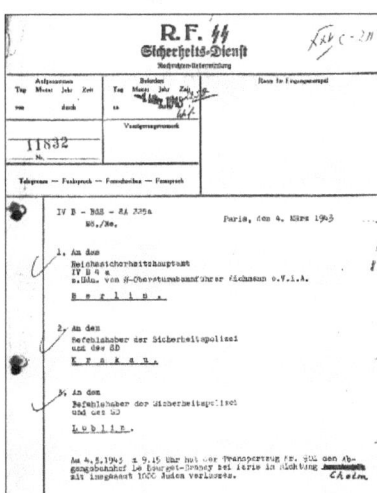

These documents, which have the information
about my grandfather's final voyage to Drancy
and Maidanek/Sobibor are on file at Yad Vashem in Jerusalem

Chapter Twenty-Nine

In my conversation with Serge Klarsfeld in 2000, he told me that my grandfather was put on Transport 50, and that if he survived the train ride to Maidanek/Sobibor, he was gassed to death upon his arrival. Martin Ruch has since told me that two other men from Gengenbach and Offenburg, Adolph Valfer and Siegfried Geismar, were also on Transport 50 with my grandfather. The German government's official date of Berthold Meier's death is March 4, 1943.

It is surely true that my grandparents didn't react quickly enough to what was happening in Germany. Even after they got to Gurs, they yearned to be back in Gengenbach. Like many Jews, their love of Germany distorted their view of what was happening to them. Through it all, they could perhaps imagine themselves living back in Germany after the Third Reich ended. When they finally woke up to the fact that their very lives depended on getting a visa and a ship's ticket, they were rejected by the State Department of the United States.

Reading the letter my father wrote to Sally and Berta Isaac shocked and saddened me when I saw that my desperate father had nearly succeeded in getting his father safely to this country. Prospective immigrants can only enter through "the golden door" that is America if they are lucky enough to be welcomed—then and now.

Including Sophie and Berthold Meier.

Chapter Thirty

Can We Do It Again?

From the moment I read the translation of the newspaper article Gerda-Marie sent me, in which I discovered that *Stolpersteine* had been placed in front of my grandparents' house in May 2009, I felt conflicted. I was thrilled and disappointed at the same time.

The story about Martin Ruch's book and what the students had done was deeply touching. At the same time, it reminded me that nobody in Gengenbach knew that Sophie and Berthold Meier had living family members—two grandchildren and a great-grandson—alive and well and living in Florida, who would have been thrilled to see the dedication of the *Stolpersteine*! The only people who would have known that fact were Helmut Breunig and Franz Blum, and they were both dead.

My excitement at discovering Martin, with his willingness to translate for me and his ability to put facts into historical context, managed to calm my disappointment for a time.

Gradually, however, my frustration at missing the placing of the *Stolpersteine* would not go away. By October 2017, I was already thinking of asking Martin whether he thought the town would rededicate the *Stolpersteine* if Jeffrey, Adam, and I traveled to Gengenbach.

At first, it seemed like a wildly insane idea—even to me. The original installation had happened nine years earlier—all of the students and some of the teachers would be gone from Marta-Schanzenbach. Most of the city officials had changed too. But when I finally got up the courage to tell Martin, bless his heart, what I was thinking, he never tried to discourage me. Instead, he set about seeing what he could do to arrange what we were soon calling a "Rededication."

In May, I received a formal letter inviting me to attend a "Rededication" of the Meier *Stolpersteine* at Grünstraße 27 at 11:30 AM on June 15, 2018!

With Martin's help and support from the town of Gengenbach,

Chapter Thirty

serendipity placed me in front of the Meier house on Grünstraße that day with Jeffrey, Adam, Dr. Martin Ruch, Gerda-Marie Lüttgen, and many wonderful people from the town, rededicating Berthold and Sophie Meier's *Stolpersteine*.

 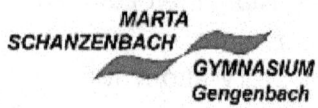

Mrs. Susan Moss Katz
8621 SW 79 Place
Miami, FL 33143
USA

Gengenbach, 09. Mai 2018

Sehr geehrte Frau Moss Katz,

Ihren Besuch in unserem schönen Gengenbach nehmen wir gerne zum Anlass im Gedenken an Ihre Großeltern, Sophie und Berthold Meier, als Opfer des Nationalsozialismus, eine kleine Feier auszurichten.

Hierzu möchten wir Sie recht herzlich am

Freitag, den 15. Juni 2018 um 11:30 Uhr,

an den "Stolpersteinen" - Wider das Vergessen,

vor dem ehemaligen Anwesen Ihrer Großeltern (Grünstraße 27), einladen.

Wir freuen uns sehr auf Ihr Kommen.

Mit freundlichen Grüßen

Thorsten Erny
Bürgermeister

Aiko Schuhmann
stellv. Schulleiter

Chapter Thirty-One

The Green Photo Album

My attachment to my father's green photo album goes back a long way. I remember him showing it to me in the attic in Pottsville, and after his death, it became a link to him and the life he had left behind. The pictures in it carried the stories of his childhood with them, but sadly, there was no way for me to retrieve the stories. I could only imagine them.

My feelings for the album became even more obvious several years ago when I noticed it was threatening to crumble. One day, as I took it out and looked sadly at the black pages that were disintegrating in front of my eyes, I realized that it was the pages themselves that were the biggest problem. The photographs, especially the oldest German ones, were often mounted on cardboard and were much sturdier—in fact, they were causing the paper that they were mounted on, using old-fashioned photo corners, to rip apart.

Chapter Thirty-One

The problem became more obvious as I began to take out my father's green photo album more often in order to make copies of pictures to send to Martin as he was doing research on the Meier family.

Meanwhile, and unrelated, I was developing a growing sense that I needed to come up with a unique gift to give the special people who were planning the rededication of the *Stolpersteine* on June 15th and inviting me to visit and/or speak.

One day it hit me—maybe I could kill two birds with one stone and make a book out of the dear old green photo album? If I had a book made from the original album, it would live on after the crumbling original ended up buried on a shelf in one of the Holocaust Museums where it was probably destined to go eventually. And, I could give copies as gifts in Germany to the people who helped to place the original *Stolpersteine* or who welcomed us for the rededication.

I began to contemplate taking the album to a place that made digital copies of old pictures. I knew there was one in South Miami, and so one day I packed up the album in its careful, diaper-like wrapping and the plastic box it lived in, and headed off to find out if what I wanted could be done. Much to my dismay, the business was gone! Then I noticed a small sign on the door which said that the business had moved to the warehouse district. Determined, I tracked it down, and when I found it, I spoke with the owner. He told me that there was a woman working there who specialized in doing just what I needed—working with old photo albums.

It turned out that I had several options. The woman could copy the pages, or she could copy the individual photographs, page by page. Naturally, the second option cost a lot more money to do. As I considered how to proceed, it occurred to me that I had a problem I had never even thought about before— the pictures were mounted in the photo album in random order! They were not placed in chronological order nor by subject matter. Photographing the pages would result in copying the disorder that had always existed. On the other hand, it would preserve the album more authentically.

Naturally, I had no idea where or how the album had originally been assembled. Did my father bring the pictures with him from Germany and then put them in the album just to preserve them when he got to America? Probably—as the album said, in English—*Photographs*. In any case, I had a big decision to make—should I tackle creating order as I made the book?

Anyone who knows me already knows the answer to what I did—I had the artist do both—first she copied the pages and then the individual pictures. My objective became to create a book that would preserve the green photo album and yet also tell a coherent story of my father's life in Germany from 1910 to 1937 that I could give as gifts to the people who were helping me.

When the woman sent me the digital pictures, I began a task that was far more arduous than I could have imagined. I spent weeks trying to organize the photographs chronologically and by subject matter! And then deciding which pictures to put on each page with captions! The difficult task gave me a familiarity with the pictures that I really did not have when I started—not so bad for writing my memoir! It reinforced, however, how few names I could still attach to most of the people in the photos, a constant reminder of the stories behind each picture that I would never know.

When I finally finished creating order out of the chaos to the best of my ability, the extremely creative woman with whom I was working produced a lovely book, capturing the spirit of the story the pictures told and which I was trying to write about in my book.

I would never dare to confess to anyone what the project cost in terms of money! In confession I will also admit that the original book had to be redone several times—later research from Martin revealed names and dates that were wrong or missing in the original book. Hopefully, the various recipients of the books will never compare their copies—the later the version, the more accurate the captions! My last confession, sadly, is that the final version still has one error—one date is still wrong. But you will have to torture me to get me to confess where the mistakes are in the photo books that sit on shelves here and in Germany that were made from the old green album.

Chapter Thirty-Two

The Rolands Appear

Since we had been working together, I had often lamented to Martin Ruch about my absolute lack of knowledge about my grandmother, Sophie Roland Meier. All I knew was that she was an only child who came from Sinsheim and that her family were Reform Jews. That's it! I had learned a great deal about the Meier family, but there was a gaping hole when it came to the Rolands. I saw what I guessed were Sophie's parents' pictures in the green photo album, but I didn't even know what their names were! My own great-grandparents!

In May, just days before I left for Gengenbach, Martin Ruch shocked me with an email containing all sorts of facts he had just gotten from Sinsheim about my grandmother's family! He had made inquiries to the city archive in Sinsheim, and he surprised me with a lot of information about the Roland family, also spelled Rolland, and to my surprise, also the Frank Family, a name I had never even heard before!

The man in the photo in the green album was indeed my great-grandfather, Adolf (Wolf) Roland, a merchant. The other picture was his wife, my great-grandmother, Jette Frank Roland.

Chapter Thirty-Two

It appears that both the Rolands and the Franks lived in that part of Germany for a long time. My grandmother's family has graves in the Jewish Cemetery in Sinsheim that go back hundreds of years.

Sadly, one of the graves was that of the man in the picture, Sophie's father, my great-grandfather, Wolf Roland, who was born on March 16, 1842 and died very young, at age 54 on October 9, 1896. He was born 100 years before I was born in 1942 and sadly, 100 years before his daughter Sophie starved to death, in January 1942 at Camp de Gurs.

What is more, I now also learned the names of Wolf's parents! His father's name was Isaak Roland, and he was born on September 2, 1809 in Sinsheim. He was a businessman who died on June 7, 1876 at the age of 66. Wolf's mother was Mina Hahn Roland, and she was born in Berwangen in 1813 and died on September 16, 1892. What is more, I even learned the names of Wolf's grandparents, Assur and Sara Levi Roland! There were birth and death records for many of the Rolands in Sinsheim.

I was thrilled that I now knew the names of all four of my great-great grandparents—Roland and Meier, thanks to Martin and his research.

Puzzled, however, I saw that Jette Frank Roland's grave was not on the list from Sinsheim. Only a record of her marriage to Adolf Roland. No death notice! That was major confusion for me for only a few days—until the day of the rededication of the *Stolpersteine*.

At the end of the celebration on June 15, 2018, the city of Gengenbach presented me with a surprise—my grandparents' marriage license. It said, *"The single Sofie Rolland, known for being of the Israelite religion, born on March 27, 1878 in Sinsheim, daughter of the deceased merchant Adolf Rolland and Jette, born Frank, living in Gengenbach."*

Reading it gave me another surprise—Jette, born Frank, living in Gengenbach???

Why was Jette Roland living in Gengenbach? Did she follow her daughter there when Sophie married Berthold Meier? Where in Gengenbach did she live? And where was she buried?

I have never gotten the answer to my first three questions, but, to my surprise, the mystery of where Jetta was buried would be solved within a few days—at the Jewish Cemetery in Offenburg.

Using a book Martin Ruch had written about the cemetery, I discovered that Jetta Frank Roland's grave was there—in the cemetery in Offenburg, and before I knew it, I was standing in front of it! What I will never know is why it is there—how did my great-grandmother end up in Gengenbach and come to be buried in Offenburg in 1914, not in Sinsheim? As I looked at her grave, the date of her death jumped out at me...January 13th. In shock, I realized that her daughter, Sophie, died on the same date, January 13th, in 1942 at Gurs. From starvation.

Chapter Thirty-Three

Where is Grünstraße 27?

Memory is a wonderful thing. On June 13, 2018, as Adam and I drove into Gengenbach, I directed him easily to Grünstraße on which my grandparents' home sits as though I had been there a short time ago. Actually it was two months shy of 50 years, since August 1968, when his father and I drove to the house where my grandfather had been born—my first and only visit to beautiful Gengenbach before this day in 2018! Since that trip, I have pictured that house often, so often that it was deeply embedded in my memory. Including how to get there.

As Adam followed my directions and drove toward the street, the feeling that I had done it only a few years earlier became greater and greater.

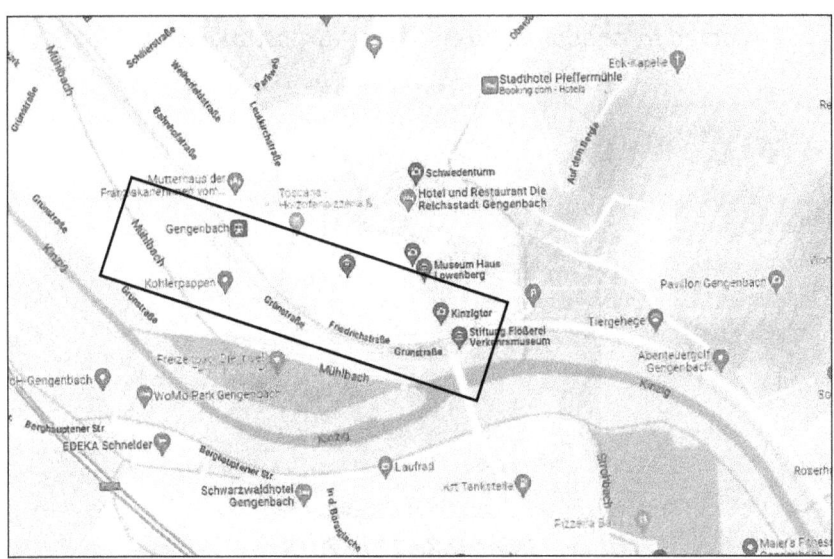

A map of the town of Gengenbach showing Grünstraße where the Meier house is located

We found Grünstraße with no problem with the Kinzig River right behind it. We drove up and down the street several times, but no house looked like the one I remembered. I was shocked

Chapter Thirty-Three

that I couldn't find the house! Finally, completely puzzled, I said, "Let's look for the house number—27."

When we found 27, I gasped! It sure didn't look like the house in the green photo album nor the house I had visited and even been inside of in 1968!

The carved front door in 1968

Grünstraße 27 in 1968

Grünstraße 27 in 2018

Not only was the beautifully carved front door frame gone, but the whole front door was also gone! Where it had been was now just a wall! The gardens around the house were gone and replaced with a new garage. While the beautiful bay window on the second floor was still a bay window, it sure wasn't beautiful anymore.

Where is Grünstraße 27?

"Well!" I said to Adam, "When I was here fifty years ago, they told me they had to do something about the wooden door frame which was rotting. Instead of repairing it, I guess they decided to get rid of it altogether. What a shame! The Meier house is so ordinary now." As I said those words I realized it was true—the house had absolutely no character or distinction anymore! I was disappointed that Adam was not seeing the charming old Meier house that I had seen before he was born.

My next shock came when we parked the car and began to walk toward the golden brass *Stolpersteine* that were in the picture I had stared at over and over again for a year. The shock was how different they looked from the way they had in the picture!

2009

2018

Chapter Thirty-Three

The once shiny brass was tarnished and sad looking. The *Stolpersteine* looked like nine-year-old unpolished brass plaques, which they were!

Adam and I spent the next two days desperately shopping for brass cleaner. I couldn't stand the thought of the rededication, with the *Stolpersteine* looking like they did! We had no luck, and finally Adam spent quite a bit of time on his hands and knees, trying to get the brass shiny using various liquids and cloths we had acquired on our unsuccessful search for brass cleaner. On the day of the ceremony, the *Stolpersteine* looked cleaner than we had found them, but not like the picture taken in 2009 at the original installation.

On June 15th, when the Meier family collected before the ceremony, it turned out that Jeffrey and I had both had the same thought. We each showed up with a small collection of personal objects that belonged to Sophie, Berthold, and our father, Arthur. When the guests arrived on the 15th, this is what they saw. The ring baked in the cookie is on the bottom right.

It gradually became apparent to me that the *Stolpersteine* represented something very special to the three remaining members of the Meier family—Jeffrey, Adam and me. They were far more than two brass plaques in front of the house on Grünstraße. They were truly memorials to Sophie and Berthold Meier: Not in Gurs where she is buried. Not at Maidanek/Sobibor where his ashes or bones are now part of a mass grave. Not at the Holocaust Memorial on Miami Beach where their names are inscribed on the wall. Their true memorials are the *Stolpersteine* in front of their beloved home at 27 Grünstraße in Gengenbach, Germany.

And, by the way, if I ever get to Gengenbach again, there will be several cans of Brasso in my luggage.

Chapter Thirty-Four

The Stolpersteine on Grünstraße

When I first got the impulse to ask Martin if he thought we could rededicate the *Stolpersteine*, I hesitated. I don't request or wish for things out of my reach very often, so asking him this would be an unusual thing for me to do. Making wishes is hard for me because I often don't have control over whether or not they will come true. One of the things I have learned about myself is that I like certainty so much that if I don't think I can win, I don't even try.

But, wish I did, and the wish that came true was even better than I imagined—thanks to some very special people, all of whom I was eagerly waiting to meet and thank on June 15, 2018.

Adam, Jeffrey, and I arrived in Gengenbach on June 13th. I will always remember the moment I met Martin Ruch when he came to see us as soon as we got to Gengenbach. I felt as though I was seeing someone I already knew—after a year of sharing many personal moments as he translated my letters, he had become a special friend.

Chapter Thirty-Four

The other person I was very excited to meet was Gerda-Marie Lüttgen, the woman who had sent me the original email which started this entire chapter of my life to begin! Gerda turned out to be a pretty, charming woman, who greeted me with the same warmth I was feeling for her. I think that the significance of our chance encounter had clearly affected both of us enormously.

The people of the town of Gengenbach had gone out of their way to make this special day very extraordinary—we were congregated where the pear trees once stood in my grandparents' garden and was now the driveway in front of the garage of the redesigned house. Someone had brought a large standing bulletin board with pictures and newspaper articles from the original 2009 dedication of the *Stolpersteine*.

A very important moment came when we met and heard from Michael Roschach, the former Mayor of Gengenbach, who had been so supportive of all the memorials that the students of the Marta-Schanzenbach-Gymnasium had created over the years, including the *Stolpersteine* in 2009.

A photographer from the Mittelbadische Presse took a picture and wrote an article for the newspaper about our celebration

During the rededication, Mayor Roschach explained his justification for the original dedication of the *Stolpersteine* by reminding the citizens that the 30 Jews living in Gengenbach in 1933 were integrated as respected citizens. But, only a little later, they were mocked, ridiculed, expelled and deported. We must never forget what happened then!

Bürgermeister Erny, the current Mayor, then began the ceremony, speaking in German, by telling the story of the Meier family. As he spoke, Vice-Chancellor Aiko Schuhmann of the school translated his message into English. The two men told the story of how the *Stolpersteine* came to exist, despite the opposition that came from some of Gengenbach's citizens. Then they told the group how, with the help of Michael Götz, the leader of the BürgerServices, I had connected with Martin Ruch. Finally, they explained what Martin and I had been doing over the past year.

Vice-Chancellor Schuhmann and two teachers, Peter Bechtold and Klaus Brenner, who had led the original *Stolpersteine* project, came with a group of their students from the Marta-Schanzenbach-Gymnasium. They had written a special presentation to share with us.

Chapter Thirty-Four

Next, Thorsten Erny and Michael Götz had beautiful gifts and surprises for us from the town. The most wonderful surprise of all was a copy of my grandparents' marriage license which I had never before seen! Sophie and Berthold Meier had married on January 25, 1909 at City Hall in Gengenbach. I kidded the group that I was very happy to discover that my grandparents had really been married and everyone laughed!

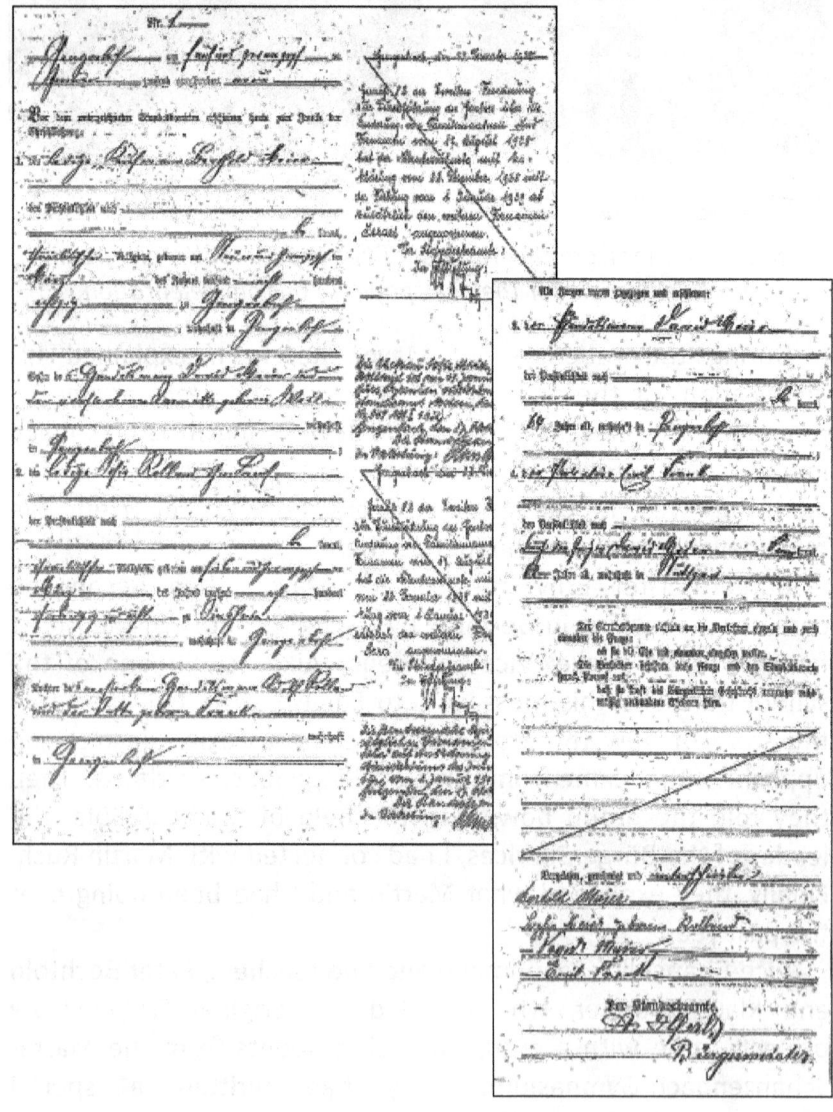

Sophie Roland Meier, my grandmother, was only 18 years old when her father, Wolf, died. She and Berthold, who was only 17 when his mother died, had that in common. So, my pressing question for both of them after reading their marriage license is—**why did you wait so long to get married?** Sophie was 31 and Berthold was 29—they were both good-looking, intelligent, from middle-class families, but both old-maids! Guess I'll never have the answer to that question.

I presented many people with gifts too. I had this very meaningful framed lithograph by Joanne Fink for Martin and certificates for trees planted in Israel for Martin and Gerda-Marie.

Chapter Thirty-Four

I was especially proud of the photo book I had made from my father's green photo album. I read the dedication to the group before I gave them as gifts.

> The pictures in this book come from the photo album that my father, Arthur Meier, carried with him on his trip to America on the S. S. President Roosevelt in August, 1937. After his death in 1954, my father's album was carefully preserved by his wife Sylvia, and later, by me.
>
> In honor of the rededication of the Stolpersteine in Gengenbach on June 15, 2018, I created a photo journal of my father's life in Gengenbach from 1910 to 1937. It is a gift from me, my brother Jeffrey Meier, and my son Adam Moss to Dr. Martin Ruch and to the teachers and students of the Marta-Schanzenbach-Gymnasium. In 2009, Dr. Ruch's book, _The Seven-Hundred Year History of the Jews of Gengenbach: 1308 – 2008_, served as an inspiration for the school to place Stolpersteine on Grünstraße in front of the home of Sophie and Berthold Meier—the house in which Arthur Meier grew up.
>
> The Meier family is grateful for this memorial and for the spirit in which the book was written and the stumbling stones were dedicated.

Never Forget

We must become the voice of those who have been silenced.

Susan Meier Moss Katz
Miami, Florida
May, 2018

My brother and I each spoke to the people gathered in the driveway in front of my grandparents' house. When I moved forward to speak, I planned to thank everyone for the beautiful celebration. Instead, with tears running down my face, I found myself saying to the group, *"For seventy-five years I have been searching for my grandparents. With your help, I have finally found them."*

The words coming out of my mouth took me by surprise! Shocked, I realized as I spoke that all these years, since Gurs, I had naively thought that my search was to find out what had happened to my grandparents. Until I said those words, I had never realized that I was actually looking for *THEM*—that I actually hoped to find *THEM*. I had thought of them as out of my reach until I found the Stolpersteine and Martin Ruch. As soon as I said the words, I realized that I had just spoken the truth. My truth. Serendipity!

At the end of the rededication, the town of Gengenbach held a lovely luncheon at the Sonne Hotel for all the guests.

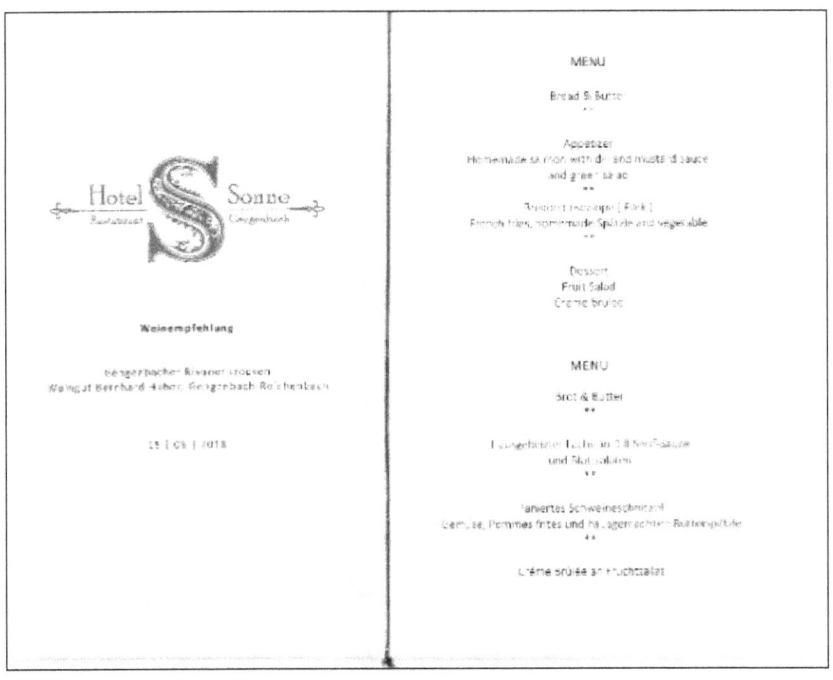

Chapter Thirty-Four

On the balcony of City Hall on Market Square, standing left to right, are Adam Moss, Michael Götz, Susan Meier Moss Katz, Mayor Thorsten Erny and Jeffrey Meier. The room just inside this balcony is more than likely where Berthold and Sophie Meier signed their marriage license.

Chapter Thirty-Five
Back to Oberrealschule

The doorway in the picture from 1930 has always intrigued me. It was the ovals set into the panels on either side that I always noticed in the photograph. And there they were—still in the same place in 2018! Nothing had changed in eighty-eight years except the name of the school—from Oberrealschule to Schiller-Gymnasium.

The class of 1930 from the Oberrealschule in Offenburg. Helmut Breunig stands on the left in the front row and Arthur Meier is the third man in the same row

Jeffrey, Susan, and Adam stand in the same door in 2018, 88 years later

Chapter Thirty-Five

How I wished my father could see us—my brother, my son, and I—standing in the doorway of the Oberrealschule in Offenburg on June 18, 2018. I knew what it would mean to him that we had come to his beloved high school. Thanks to Martin, we were warmly welcomed.

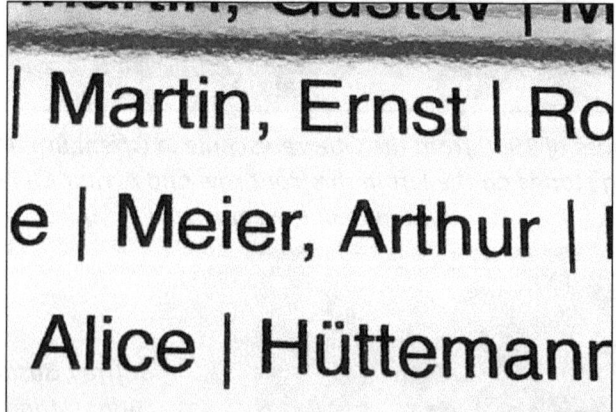

We were thrilled to have the opportunity to meet Alois Lienhard, the former Deputy Head of School, the man whose idea it was to create the glass wall with the names of all the graduates, including that of our father and grandfather, Arthur

Meier. Seeing his name on the window of graduates from the class of 1930 was a very moving moment. It was so grounded in reality for the three of us, not something we often got to experience in the case of my father.

It was also very important to me to talk to the faculty members who plan the annual October memorial. Since Martin and I connected, he has been sending me copies of the newspaper articles about the annual school project to remember the October Deportation of the Jews of Offenburg and the surrounding towns to Gurs in 1940.

Martin had arranged with Dr. Christine Schmitt, the Head of the History Department, for us to speak with some of the students at the school who had taken part in some of these October commemorations.

Dr. Schmidt's students were very interested in the story of how my father had had to leave Germany and to get our reaction to what happened to our grandparents. They were eager to ask us how we felt about coming to Germany. It was obvious that these students had studied history and it was impressive that they knew about the history of the Holocaust. They had taken part in the school's October memorial to the Jews in prior years.

The 2017 commemoration to the Deportation involved shoes in the gymnasium marking the place where the Jews had been detained until the train to Gurs came

Chapter Thirty-Five

The Schiller students also wanted to know what our father had told us about his days at the school. I did not have the heart to tell them that my father had died so young, when his children were so young as well, that we didn't have time to talk about his school days. Luckily, I had brought them a copy of several wonderful pictures and drawings from my father's days at Oberrealschule. I shared with them that there was so much evidence in the green photo album that it was obvious that the school was dear to his heart. I also told them how he and Helmut Breunig, his dear friend, and all the other students from Gengenbach rode the train back and forth each day to attend the school in Offenburg.

An article about my grandparents, written by Martin Ruch, was in the newspaper in conjunction with that year's memorial at Schiller

For Jeffrey, Adam, and me this day was really special. There had been so few other moments in our lives that made our father/grandfather seem real to us because he had been a part of our lives for such a short time. Sometimes Jeffrey and I felt as though we had never really known him. As for Adam, he grew up with no living grandfathers, so it must have been doubly hard for him to imagine my father. But that day, at Oberrealschule, reminded us that we had not imagined Arthur Meier after all. He was a real schoolboy at this special place.

Chapter Thirty-Six

The Stench of Evil

There was one more thing on our "to-do" list at the school—the thing I most dreaded. As we walked toward the Schillersaal, now the gymnasium of the Schiller School, where my grandparents had spent their last hours in Germany before boarding the train to Gurs, I could feel my feet beginning to slow down. Adam, Jeffrey, and the three teachers from the school got to the door before I did, opened it, and walked in. I stopped in the doorway and looked in. I had tried to envision this gymnasium ever since I found out what happened here in Offenburg on October 22, 1940. Now I was about to set foot in this dreadful room.

Frozen in place, I just watched the others walk in and look around at the beautiful parquet floor, the high walls with large windows in them, and the ceiling, which curved on either side to meet the walls. A large, sun-filled attractive room, for sure, but the stench of evil burned my nose, and I began to weep.

I waited in the doorway until the group moved out. Then I walked in slowly and stopped. I stood there, picturing the room filled with 116 souls, many of them older men and women, terrified about what had already happened to them that morning and completely uncertain about what would come next. I was sure that the Nazis did not provide them with chairs, and, so, I pictured them sitting on the wooden floor or on the one suitcase they were each allowed to take with them. Many of them must have known each other; they had been rounded up in the small towns around Offenburg and brought here to the Schillersaal in trucks by the SS. A fair number of them were probably even somehow related to each other—this part of Germany contained a Jewish community that traced its roots back many generations and there must have been a lot of intermarrying within their families. These 116 men and women and children had all been awakened from their sleep during the night, given one hour or less to pack a suitcase, 100 Marks, and be ready to get in

Chapter Thirty-Six

the trucks waiting in front of the "Jew House" in each town. I wondered how many of them had even had the time to pack a little food. The Nazis didn't provide them with that either. No chairs, no food. And no idea of what was coming next.

As I gazed around the room, however, my painful dilemma was that I KNEW how the story ended. I KNEW what would happen after they left this room. Now I could not just smell the evil—I could see it too.

After hours in this room, the mostly elderly Jews were forced to march to the railway station. At the Offenburg train station, the SS put the group on a train that had originally come from Konstanz, traveled north to Singen, Donaueschingen, Villingen, and finally Offenburg. As they climbed on the train, they heard the SS shouting...*the limit of 100 Marks must be absolutely observed. Anyone found with more will be shot immediately!*

And then, the four-day-long, hellish train ride to Gurs...

I wiped my eyes, blew my nose, and turned and walked out of the Schillersaal. Visiting this place was a seminal moment for me in my quest for the truth about Berthold and Sophie Meier. Now I had seen and smelled the evil they had been subjected to.

The Stench of Evil

The Offenburg Schillersaal as it appears in June 2018. Today it is the gymnasium of the Schiller school, once the "Oberrealschule" from which Arthur Meier graduated in 1930. It is the room to which the Jews from the towns around Offenburg were brought on October 22, 1940 by the SS to wait for the train that would take them to Camp de Gurs in France, from which few of them would ever return.

Chapter Thirty-Six

These pictures on the wall of the small Holocaust memorial in Der Salmen, once the Offenburg Synagogue, are of the 116 Jews from Offenburg and the nearby towns in Baden who were taken from their homes on October 22, 1940 and sent to the Schillersaal to wait for the train to Gurs. They were victims of the diabolical Nazi plan called The Wagner-Bürckel-Aktion, one of the earliest creations resulting from the Nazi frustration over the fact that the Jews did not all leave when they were "encouraged" to do so after Kristallnacht. It is one of the first attempts to expel the Jews from Germany and ghettoize them in a foreign country.

The Nazis put these Jews, many elderly, on the train at the station in Offenburg. From there, they traveled to Camp de Gurs in southern France. It was possible to leave Gurs only if one had the money to do so and a place to go that would take you in. Many men, women, and children died at Gurs—from starvation or illness or suicide. Most of them never left. Those who survived were eventually sent to Drancy and from there to Auschwitz or Maidanek/Sobibor, where they were gassed upon their arrival.

The Stench of Evil

The woman and man at the top of the center row, under the arrow, are Sophie and Berthold Meier, my grandparents. Sophie died of starvation at Gurs on January 13, 1942. She is buried in the cemetery there. Berthold survived and was sent to Drancy and from there east on Transport 50 to Maidanek/Sobibor, where, if he survived the train ride he was gassed to death on his arrival. His death is officially recorded as March 4, 1943.

It is also entirely possible that among these pictures is Berthold's younger sister, Elise Meier Daube, and her husband Louis, from Pforzheim. If the Daubes are not among the people in the Schillersaal, then Berthold would have met up with his sister on the train or upon his arrival at the camp. He refers to his sister, Elise, in many of his letters from Gurs, as well as to other relatives and friends. Louis Daube died early on at Gurs. Elise survived Gurs, but eventually was sent to Auschwitz, where most of the occupants of Gurs ended up. Elise's death is officially recorded by the German government as December 4, 1942. The Daubes are remembered with Stolpersteine placed in front of their home at 33 Jahnstraße in Pforzheim.

Chapter Thirty-Seven

Bonbons Redux

In the Grünstraße lived Mr. Meier, a small fat man with a goatee. He was a salesman in tobacco goods, and he always had bonbons for us children. He, too, came into our business because he was, of course, a Gengenbacher like us.

Annemie Sewald
<u>700 Years of Jewish Life in Gengenbach – 1308 to 2008</u>
Dr. Martin Ruch

Dr. Martin Ruch's book, <u>700 years of Jews in Gengenbach 1308-2008</u>

When Martin sent me a copy of the information he had written about my grandparents in his book and I read what Annemie Sewald, a woman who had actually known Berthold Meier and was still alive, told him about my grandfather, I became desperate to meet her. She was 89 years old, so the

Chapter Thirty-Seven

chance to talk with her might not exist much longer. The minute we finalized our trip to Gengenbach, Martin arranged a meeting with her at her home for Saturday, June 16th, the day after the *Stolpersteine* rededication. I quickly built up in my mind all kinds of things she might tell me about my grandfather.

When we drove up to her house, we found that Annemie Sewald was outside waiting for us. She was amazingly spry and alert for an 89-year-old. She led us up the steps to her thoroughly modern house and into her dining room. We were all invited to sit around the dining room table. When we were settled and Martin had made the introductions, I handed Annemie the box of chocolates I had brought from Miami. She read my note which said in German, "Here are bonbons once again from the Meier family." She accepted them graciously, but it seemed to me that she was not getting the connection between the candy I had brought with me, to what she had told Martin about my grandfather always giving bonbons to the children of Gengenbach.

Martin must have sensed the disconnect too, because he took out his book and read the part where she had talked about my grandfather and the bonbons. She nodded and said, "Yes, I always loved sweets." I do not think she ever got the intended symbolism of the fact that we were recreating something my grandfather had done in the 1930s and which she had remembered and told Martin about. I didn't care—it still felt like it was the perfect gift to have brought her!

Annemie Sewald with her box of bonbons from the Meier family in 2018

Annemie's English was not very good, so all of this took place with Martin translating. Next, I handed her a photograph of my grandfather with five of the village children. It came from my father's photo album, and I had blown it up into an 8 X 10 print. I was hoping that even if she wasn't one of the children, she would at least recognize someone in the photo. Again, I struck out. She even used a magnifying glass to look at the faces, but it was clear she really didn't know or remember any of them. The only person she recognized in the picture was my grandfather. That was no surprise. I felt like we had hit another dead end.

Berthold Meier surrounded by neighbor children in Gengenbach

Annemie got up from the table and went off to get a box of photos and some albums to show us something, but she never did find what it was she was looking for. She came back to the table empty-handed. By this time, I was feeling really let down. This visit was not adding anything to my quest to find out more about my grandparents, which is why I had come to see her. I felt a growing impatience, and finally signaled to Martin that I thought we should go.

Just then, one of us, although I can't remember who, mentioned the morning of October 22, 1940, when the Gestapo

Chapter Thirty-Seven

came to get the Jews left in Gengenbach for the round-up, their truck ride to Offenburg, their day in the Schillersaal, and the subsequent train ride to Camp de Gurs in southern France. Suddenly, Annemie became quite animated as she began to describe how she and her family saw the whole thing from the window of their house. She described a man with a young son who were watching as my grandparents and the other Jews were loaded onto the trucks. The man lifted his son onto his shoulders so he could see better. As the truck drove away, he gleefully said to the boy, "Look! There you see the last Gengenbach Jews!" She said that this experience was so drastic that her memory of it has not faded to this day.

As she was talking, the hair on my arms began to stand on end, and I suddenly found it hard to breathe. You see, in a chapter I had already written months ago about that October day in 1940, I had created a story based on a real photograph I had seen, taken in Kippenheim on the morning of October 22, 1940. In the real photo, a child is seen standing in the foreground, watching the Jews being loaded onto a truck. In MY story, I had named the young child observing the scene in Gengenbach "Annemie Sewald" because that was literally the only person from the town whose name I knew and who had been the right age to have been the child in the photograph. When I invented that connection, I had no idea she had actually witnessed the events taking place in front of the Judenhaus that morning! What I had accidentally recreated as fiction had much more truth in it than I knew. I still think of Chapter 17 as semi-fictional, but truthfully, it is remarkably close to Annemie's truthful and painful memory of that morning.

It was not the moment to stop Annemie's recollection nor to confront the group at the table with the astounding coincidence that I had accidentally created. But it suddenly made the conversation around the table into one of the most important moments of the week for me.

The discussion moved next to how difficult it was for the residents of Gengenbach after the Nuremburg Laws were passed in 1933. Annemie described how SS guards stood in front of

Jewish shops so no one could go in and buy from them. The Jews they had known all their lives, like my grandfather, were now *Untermenschen**.

> **Untermenschen means subhuman, a term that became infamous when the Nazis used it to describe non-Aryan "inferior people" often referred to as "the masses from the East," Jews and Slavs (mainly ethnic Poles, Serbs, and later Russians). The term was also applied to most Blacks and persons of color, as well to Romani people (gypsies), homosexuals, and the physically and mentally disabled. According to the Generalplan Ost, the concept of extermination of Untermenschen was an important part of the Nazi racial policy.*

I reminded Martin of the postcard he had translated written by my father in 1937 while he was in Paris waiting to board the ship. He was writing in eager anticipation to his Uncle Emil who was waiting for him in America, and he used the word, "Pigsty," to describe what Germany had become. Martin and I had been very intrigued by the word choice my father used to describe what he was leaving. After listening to Annemie, I better understood his word choice.

Annemie told the story of how her grandfather and father were butchers, used to accommodating the Jews of Gengenbach by observing rules of "Kashrut," kosher law, when killing animals for them. These laws included severing the jugular vein, so the animal dies instantly and not slowly and in pain. A Jewish family, regular customers, needed meat after Annemie's family was no longer allowed to sell to them. Her father bravely killed a goat for them, anyway, using the required kosher method. To cover up his crime, her father then severed the entire head off the goat before giving the rest of the animal to the Jews. Next, he shot the goat's head between the eyes, and then he put the head in a barrel.

Sure enough, the Gestapo showed up quickly, demanding to know if he had killed an animal in a kosher way for a Jew. When her father produced the goat's head from the barrel, with the bullet hole in its forehead, they left.

Chapter Thirty-Seven

To me, this was a touching example of the "good" people of Gengenbach my father had told me about years earlier. It showed the conflict some Germans lived with after the Nazis came to power.

Annemie described how frightening it was for her as a young girl and how vulnerable she was with her blond hair and blue eyes. The Germans were very interested in children her age and worked hard to indoctrinate them into the Nazi culture. Instead of going to church on Sundays as they had always done, the children were forced to go to the cinema to watch propaganda films. The children were required to wear uniforms to make them feel as though they were important members of the regime.

Annemie also said she had to ride the train daily to an SS school in Offenburg and that she remembered being required to draw anti-Semitic cartoons in school. Martin explained to us that virulent anti-Semitic cartoons were one of the most common ways the Nazis spread hatred of the Jews throughout Europe. He explained that some of the most famous cartoons were published in a magazine called "Der Stürmer." I nodded my head—I had seen some of these dreadful cartoons in "Der Stürmer" at the Holocaust Museum in Nuremberg on my river cruise a year earlier.

Annemie told us that when she thinks back to that time, the feeling she gets is one of terrible fear. Even after the war, when Gengenbach was part of the French Zone*, life for a pretty teenage German girl was very unsafe. One time, she told us, she had to wade into the Kinzig River to hide from some guards who were walking toward her. She was ultimately rescued by a couple from the village who saw her and helped her climb out of the river and go home.

*The Allies divided Germany into four zones after their victory in WWII—French, American, English, and Russian. The idea was to be able to more closely control the activities of the Germans. The part of Baden that included Gengenbach and Offenburg was part of the French Zone, with a population of 1.2 million people. The French Zone designation lasted until 1949.

We spent about two hours with Annemie Sewald—the only person left we would ever meet who knew my grandfather, Berthold Meier, and who could also bear witness to life in Gengenbach from 1930 to today.

But for me, there was one additional treat—I got to meet one of the characters in my book who had actually come alive and spent two hours talking to me!

And I got to give her bonbons from the Meier family again.

Chapter Thirty-Eight

A Day in Heaven

The plans for our stay in Germany after the rededication of the *Stolpersteine* were loosely constructed. Martin seemed to be putting things in order as we went. I was not in charge, and since I trusted him, I pretty much went along with what he arranged. I knew we were going to meet the woman who had known my grandfather on Saturday and to the Schiller-Gymnasium in Offenburg on Monday, a must on my list, but beyond that, I was so thrilled with the way things were working out that I really did not have much left I was wishing for.

Meanwhile, Jeffrey apparently had some plans of his own that he was hatching. It turned out that he wanted to go to the Mercedes Museum in Stuttgart, and he wanted Adam to go with him and do the driving. I think that by Sunday, June 17th, they were both ready for a break from nostalgia and sentiment, and so they made plans to drive to Stuttgart that day. I had no desire to join them, plus I thought it would be nice if they spent some time alone together, so I planned on walking around Gengenbach, seeing what I had missed. However, that was not to be. Martin and Karoline Ruch had other surprise plans for me. They told me they would pick me up on Sunday morning, and so they did.

The first place we drove to was Diersburg. One of the earliest surprises Martin had had for me when we started working together was a page from the Book of Birth from Diersburg, dated June 29, 1844, which described the birth of my great-grandfather, David Meier! This village near Gengenbach is where my family apparently lived, at least in 1844.

There were many remnants left from the Jewish population of Diersburg. Although I had no idea when or where the Meier family lived, I could see the buildings where the Jews of the town lived, prayed, and were buried.

Chapter Thirty-Eight

The Jewish Cemetery in Diersburg

The Synagogue in Diersburg

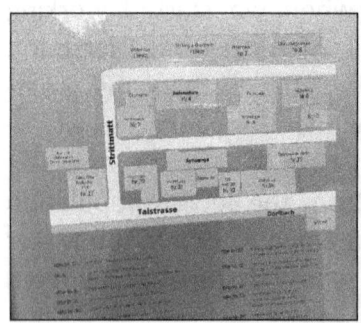
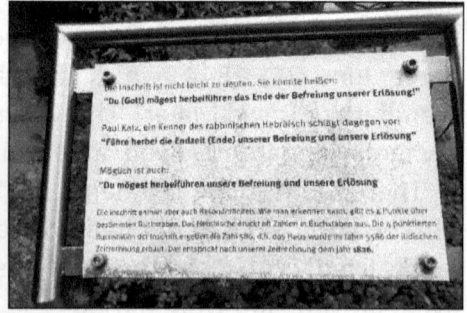

Other memorials to the Jews who lived in Diersburg before the Nazi Occupation

A Day in Heaven

It was a remarkable experience, visiting the town where my great-grandfather had been born, 174 years earlier, almost to the day!

As we drove out of Diersburg, I asked Martin and Karoline where we were going next, and they explained that Gerda-Marie and her husband Franz had invited us to visit them in Offenburg. I was delighted because I had had only a short time to speak with Gerda-Marie at the luncheon on Friday and I had never met her husband. This lady is and always will be very special to me because it was her email that started the whole remarkable experience! And I still consider it serendipity that made me add her name to the original email I sent to Gunther Demnig.

We drove to Offenburg, went through the town, and then we began to climb a hill on the outskirts of the city. It turned out that their lovely house was on the side of a hill, above which rose a beautiful vineyard. They welcomed us warmly and led us to a charming terrace behind their house with a table set for a meal.

When I tell you the next two hours were heaven, I am not exaggerating. We ate a wonderful fruit dessert that Gerda had made, drank coffee and tea, and talked about many things— from my visit to Germany to the world situation. I was sitting

Chapter Thirty-Eight

in heaven with four remarkably caring and bright people, two of whom had changed my life forever—Gerda-Marie and Martin. I felt like I was in a wonderful dream. I found myself wishing that time would stop so this moment would last forever. It didn't, of course, and can never be recreated. Time has moved on. But for me, June 17, 2018, was a day in heaven.

Chapter Thirty-Nine

Forgiveness

Remembering our history has always been an important part of the Jewish tradition. That being said, I have long known that there are people who do not understand how I could possibly have any interest in my father's German past. Surely a Jew like me could not have the desire to look back and find anything of interest about the country that gave birth to the Holocaust in which my grandparents died, and certainly not enough to write a book about it! Well, the truth is—I do! One explanation for my interest is that while I spent a paltry eleven years with my father before he died, I was left with an impression of the deep love which he had for the country of his birth and especially for his hometown of Gengenbach and for the people with whom he grew up. Unfortunately, I did not have the experience of having a conversation with my father about the contradictions he must have felt about having to escape for his life from Germany and yet still have such a warm feeling for the place where he grew up and the people in his past, which he appeared to have in the short time he was in my life.

The only contemporary proof I have about his love and affection for his hometown occurred on my first visit to Gengenbach in 1968. When I was invited into the Meier house, there was a woman from the house next door waiting for me when I came out. She had seen me when I arrived, recognized me as Arthur's daughter, and waited outside to say hello. She recognized me because my father had sent her pictures of me as a child and because I looked like him! She told me that during the years after the war, while Gengenbach was in the French Zone and consumer products were in scarce supply, my father had mailed my baby clothes to her to use for her little girl!

Martin Ruch also tells and writes about Jews from Offenburg who return to visit regularly.

And so, I engaged in research about the Meier family, worked with Martin Ruch, and planned for the *Stolpersteine*

Chapter Thirty-Nine

rededication, all with a positive outlook about what I was doing. My eyes, however, were wide open to the fact that in Germany today there is, in the words of New York Times writer, James Angelos, "...a phenomenon that came to be known as *secondary anti-Semitism,* in which Germans resent Jews for reminding them of their guilt, reversing the victim and perpetrator roles."

My personal belief about anti-Semitism is that it is an obscenity which has been around from the beginning of time, long before anyone ever heard of Adolf Hitler, and that it continues to this moment in time. And, sadly, that it will threaten the Jews forever, wherever they are. With my family history, anti-Semitism has haunted me my whole life. The question to me is only: When will anti-Semitism be quiet and when will it roar into full force?

The need for the Germans to find someone to blame after their tremendous loss and humiliation in World War I turned out to be a watershed moment for them to turn on and, finally, to kill the Jews, just as the Spanish had done during the Inquisition. First, the book burning, and then the killing, all the while keeping silent—history repeats itself regularly.

I learned and wrote about my German heritage without dealing with the belief that I had to accept forgiveness—only the victims could have done that—and they are all dead.

In the words of Daniel Mendelsohn in <u>Before the Holocaust Fades Away</u>, I belong to *"...the last generation that will be touched personally by the Holocaust, the last for whom it will be more than a matter of intellectual or historical interest or of moral inquiry. There is, in our relationship to the event, a strange interweaving of tantalizing proximity and unbridgeable distance. We are the last generation to whom the dead are close enough to touch, yet frustratingly out of reach."*

In <u>The Sunflower</u>, Simon Wiesenthal presents us with the dilemma he faced—should he have forgiven the confession of the dying young Nazi? Was his silence an act of forgiving? Wiesenthal concludes that "...forgiveness is an act of volition, and only the sufferer is qualified to make that decision."

Among the responses to Wiesenthal's question in <u>The Sunflower</u> is one from Abraham J. Heschel, the famous Rabbi and Teacher. Heschel said, *"...preposterous to assume that anybody alive can extend forgiveness for the suffering of anyone of the six million people who perished. According to Jewish tradition, even God himself can only forgive crimes committed against Himself, not against man."*

I do not ever use the word "forgiving" to describe my attitude toward Germans. I do not want to leave anyone with the impression that I forgive what the Nazis did. I don't. My own personal philosophy is that I cannot forgive what was done to my father and grandparents. I was not one of the victims—they were. Therefore, only they could forgive. For myself, I believe that the atrocities committed by the Nazis were too terrible ever to be forgiven.

How then can I have a positive attitude toward Germany and Germans, given what happened to my father and my grandparents? The reason for this is because I do not believe that all of the Germans were Nazis. I believe that the people of Gengenbach in the 1930s fell into three groups:

- One group of people was very happy to help the Nazis exterminate the Jews, whom they had always hated.
- A second group did not like the terrible laws being passed by the Nazis but were afraid to disobey them because they were afraid for themselves and their families—to take the side of the victims would have been an unsafe thing to do.
- The final group of people were good human beings and did whatever they could to support or rescue Jews as bad things began to happen, sometimes risking their own lives.

It seems to me that the act of studying Martin Ruch's book and doing the *Stolpersteine* project in 2009 was a very positive way for the school children from the Marta-Schanzenbach-Gymnasium in Gengenbach to deal with history, especially for young people. When I learned about it, I was deeply touched by what had been done by Dr. Ruch, the city, the school, the

Chapter Thirty-Nine

teachers, and the students. I only wished to recreate the beautiful remembrance of the Meier family by repeating the dedication of the Stolpersteine with the remaining family members, including me, there as witnesses. Thus, when I contacted the city and school, it was to see if I could do just that.

The welcome which my son, my brother, and I received on June 15th reinforced my belief that there always were, and hopefully always will be, people who are good human beings. The people who helped with this special ceremony were respectful of the history of my family AND of the history of the Holocaust. It does not mean that there were not people in Gengenbach who were Nazis in the 1930s nor who opposed the *Stolpersteine* project in 2009 nor who avoided joining us on June 15th for the same reason. My positive attitude comes from the fact there are people then and now who are good human beings. They showed up.

Because I have become the archivist for the Meier family story and am writing their history, I am bringing up the topic of my attitude toward forgiving. I think it is important that I be careful with the impression I leave when I speak about my German Meier family. By trying to remember how they lived, I hope to avenge my family's deaths by not allowing them to be forgotten. Perhaps you will read what I wrote and remember my family—Berthold and Sophie and Arthur Meier. My book is about remembering, not about forgiving.

In the past, I did not see myself as a spokesperson for the grandchildren of the Holocaust. Now I do.

Chapter Forty

My Fatal Obsession

Incongruous as it may seem, my fear and avoidance of the Holocaust stands in direct contradiction to my obsession with cemeteries. That's right—cemeteries. My dear friend, Rabbi Alan Weitzman, often kidded me about it, but he was right, and whatever caused my obsession, it has been with me as long as I can remember.

Perhaps it began with the trauma of my father's death on March 8, 1954. When he died, my mother's family bought an entire hill in the Orthodox cemetery in Reading. It was close to where my maternal grandparents were buried and was surrounded on all sides by extended family members from my grandmother's large Rudolph family. My family members bought a plot big enough for all seven of the children and their spouses. My father was the lone grave until my Uncle Dave died about ten years later. And now, of course, the Wise family plot is completely occupied.

I don't remember my father's actual burial in the cemetery—all I remember from that day are two things. The first was that on the macadam parking lot of the funeral home, I dropped and broke a mirror on my way into the funeral. Superstition says that a broken mirror means bad luck is coming. Truthfully, I think the bad luck had already arrived. The second thing I remember is that when I saw my father's coffin, I started screaming. Somebody hushed me up fast and told me to stop crying because I needed to be strong for my mother. Really! I'm not making that up! Today, they would have hustled me off to a psychologist to deal with my grief. Not in 1954!

From then on, we made pilgrimages to the Orthodox cemetery for the Jewish holidays and Veteran's Day, when there was always a small American flag at my father's grave because he had been in the Army. My mother outlived my father by 58 years, and when she was buried next to him in 2012, I felt a sense of closure and comfort that they were finally together again.

Chapter Forty

My parents' graves in the Orthodox Cemetery in Reading, Pennsylvania

There was one other grave we sometimes visited—Uncle Emil's—outside the fence of the Reform Cemetery in Reading. The Reform Temple had made a concession and allowed my father to have his uncle, who had committed suicide, buried outside the cemetery wall in 1938.

In the 1990s, Irwin and I visited my cousins Bobby and Kaye in Reading. They asked me if I would go with them to the Reform Cemetery to see where their recently purchased burial plots were. "Sure," I said, "then I can show Uncle Emil's grave to Irwin." Bobby and Kaye looked puzzled, so I reminded them about my father's uncle, the one who had committed suicide in 1938 and was buried outside the fence.

After looking at their new gravesite, we circled the perimeter twice looking for Emil's tombstone. "He was here!" I told them. "We used to visit his grave when I was a kid." While I discussed the mystery with Bobby and Kaye, Irwin wandered off inside the cemetery. Soon, I heard him call my name. He was standing right in the center of the cemetery. We all walked over to him, and sure enough, he was standing in front of Emil Meier's weathered grave.

"How did Uncle Emil get into the cemetery?" I asked in amazement.

My cousin Bobby suddenly got a knowing look on his face. "The Temple bought more land years ago, enlarged the cemetery, and moved the fence!

And that's how Uncle Emil moved into the cemetery.

Any wonder that I am obsessed with cemeteries?

Another unseen but compelling grave was my grandmother Sophie Meier's grave at Camp de Gurs—supposedly in a cemetery I couldn't even imagine, on the other side of the world in the Pyrenees Mountains in southern France! I had known the story of her death and burial from the time I was a little girl. I never realized until I went there in 2000 how much that cemetery and mystical grave had always subconsciously haunted me.

Chapter Forty

I will always be grateful to Irwin, because without his urging and organization, I know I would probably never have made the trip to Gurs. In the cemetery there, surrounded by all those German graves, including my grandmother's, which was right where it was supposed to be, I began to feel a curiosity to find out how Berthold and Sophie Meier actually got to Gurs in the south of France and why Sophie ended up dying there. This made it possible for me to finally want to begin to deal with the truth about what happened to my grandparents.

I thought I hit rock bottom in that cemetery. I thought I had seen the worst. But I was wrong.

We were on a Greek cruise with friends in May 2015 when my husband, Irwin, got sick, and we had get off the ship in Chania, Crete, a Greek island, where he was put in a hospital. He died suddenly two days later. "Mrs. Katz, your husband is dead." was how I was told about what happened to him. Getting him home to Miami to be buried became my frantic goal. Alone in a foreign country and deeply in shock, it was all that mattered to me. By phone, I charged my son Adam with finding a tree-shaded double plot, in the Beth Am Cemetery. It took a week, but Irwin's body and I flew from Crete to Athens to London to Miami together. Two days later I buried him in a tree-shaded plot in Miami.

I derive comfort visiting Irwin's grave occasionally. I know that his tombstone is only marking where his bones lie, but I feel like it is a connection to my memories of him. And it is, of course, where I will someday lie next to him.

With Martin Ruch's help, on our visit to the Jewish Cemetery in Offenburg in 2018, my brother, my son, and I saw the graves of three of our great-grandparents who are buried there—David and Jeanette Weil Meier and Jette Frank Roland.

I suspect that I have discovered a truth about why the *Stolpersteine* that Gunter Demnig has placed all over Europe mean so much to so many people. For many Jews, whose family members died in concentration camps and whose remains ended up in piles with many other Jewish souls' ashes and bones, there is no place to go and visit a grave. There is no point in looking in a cemetery for someone who was never buried.

What Jeffrey and Adam and I did when we rededicated our grandparents' *Stolpersteine* in Gengenbach in 2018 was a revelation to me of just how special Gunter Demnig's project is. I have heard people disparage his brass plaques as a commercial venture. To the contrary—for the Meier family and perhaps for others—it is a blessing. I realized that here was finally a memorial to Grandpa Berthold—the grave he never had and never will have. We could never find Berthold's remains at Maidanek/Sobibor, so now, finally, there is a place to pay our respects to him.

Recently, it seems that many Americans, including Jews, have begun to use cremation for their loved ones. Some people I know have scattered the ashes at favorite places of the deceased person's, and some have kept the ashes at home in an urn. Or

Chapter Forty

divvied the ashes out to their children, keeping a portion for themselves. That's not for me...especially with a grandfather who was gassed at Maidanek/Sobibor and then perhaps burned in an oven.

I have come to understand that, for me, cemeteries are an important connection to the people I lost or never knew. They always were, and still are, my link to the past. Cemeteries bring me comfort; they help me deal with my losses. Cemeteries give me a sense of posterity. Cemeteries are a home for the dead, but they are also a place where the living can visit with those who are otherwise out of reach.

Until they invent eternal life, I'm going to have to stick with cemeteries. After all, as Alan said, they are my obsession, and I am too old to find a new one now.

Chapter Forty-One

The Hero of the Story

> *We do not have to become heroes overnight. Just a step at a time, meeting each thing that comes up … discovering we have the strength to stare it down.*
> Eleanor Roosevelt
<u>You Learn by Living:</u>
<u>Eleven Keys for a More Fulfilling Life</u>

As I researched and wrote what is a deeply tragic story, a thought frequently nagged at me—one person in the story kept peeking out at me…in *heroic* fashion. As I did my research and wrote this book, as I read the letters Martin translated for me, as I poured over pictures in the green photo album, as I pieced together the timeline of the Meier family, and, finally, as I spoke to Annemie Sewald in 2018, it became obvious to me that Berthold Meier, my grandfather, is truly the remarkable *hero* of my story. The *hero* of a *memoir*? Yes!

My grandfather survived so many ironic twists of fate in his life that his story is quite unbelievable. What should have been a predictable life became like the bends in a roller coaster, each leading to unspeakable circumstances—a life filled with meeting challenges that each ultimately ended so tragically. In fact, when you read about Berthold Meier in my book, you might well ask with skepticism, don't you mean *victim* and not hero? No, I mean *hero*. *Heroes* rise above their circumstances—*staring down each thing that comes their way.*

My grandfather's positive, optimistic spirit, tremendous courage, and his strength triumphed, no matter what life handed out—in the French prisoner-of-war camp, at Dachau, Gurs, Récébédou, Camp de Nexon, Drancy, Maidanek and maybe even Sobibor. His sense of humor, his authentic love and caring for others, and his resiliency prevailed through it all. Although I only know him from his letters and the one recollection I heard about him from Annemie Sewald, I have come, over time, to feel

Chapter Forty-One

like Berthold Meier is real to me, as though I had actually met him. Because of the remarkably honest thoughts he shared in his letters, I feel like they were written to me. I feel his love.

Berthold Meier was born in Gengenbach, Germany on March 29, 1880. He was the middle of five children born to Jeanette and David Meier. He spent his childhood in the house on Grünstraße, learning the tobacco business from his father. Sadly, his mother died when he was only 17 years old. On January 25, 1909, he married Sophie Roland, an only child from a comfortable Jewish family from Sinsheim. For some reason, both the bride and groom were rather old to be marrying for the first time. Their only child, Arthur, was born on July 24, 1910.

Berthold Meier

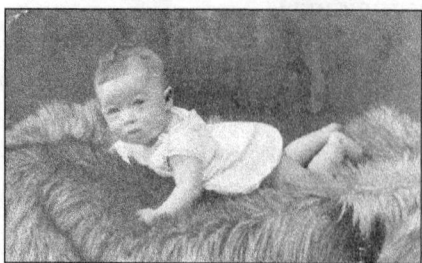

Baby Arthur

When Berthold Meier was 35 years old, he was drafted by the German Army to fight in World War I and was soon captured by the French. He spent about five years in a prison camp in France as a German soldier—years while his little son grew into a school boy in his absence. Five years, during which his beloved father, David, died.

Berthold Meier, seated on the left, in the French prisoner of war camp

For eighteen years after he came home, Berthold Meier continued his life in Gengenbach and became the man Annemie Sewald described in Martin Ruch's book—the kindly man who was remembered for handing out bonbons to the village children.

In 1938, after Kristallnacht, Berthold, and all of the male Jews of Gengenbach were arrested and spent a month at Dachau as punishment. Their release was predicated on their promises to leave Germany on their return home. Soon afterward, they were forced to give up all their valuables and Berthold had to sell his beloved family home on Grünstraße.

In an unbelievably bizarre case of irony, twenty years after being released from the French prisoner of war camp as a German soldier, Berthold Meier ended up back in France in 1939 as a prisoner of the Nazis when the Jews of Baden were sent to Camp de Gurs. The same Germans he had fought for in the First World War were now his captors in the dreadful camp in southern France. His contributions to his country were

Chapter Forty-One

totally forgotten. Adolf Eichmann watched with glee as the train carrying Berthold, his wife Sophie, and his sister Elise crossed the border into France.

Berthold, by nature resilient, must have become a survivor, who perhaps first developed his skills in his days in the prison camp in France. His experience at surviving stood him in good stead as he used it again at Gurs. In his letters he tells how he helped in the kitchen, which meant that he got a double portion of food. He often hid food in his now too-large pants to take to his wife. He served food to the barracks, including his own, and described in a letter that *"something always falls off, even if it is not much."* It didn't help enough—on January 13, 1942, his wife Sophie Meier died of starvation, and he attended her funeral in the cemetery at Gurs and then wrote to his son to tell him the news.

My enterprising grandfather did whatever needed to be done to survive at Gurs. *"My work is varied, but I like to do it. It keeps me from feeling hungry. I am also a tailor—sewing and mending, a sawmill worker, and a washerwoman."* He even made ovens from tin cans for the other refugees who used them to make coffee or soup.

Rereading his letters, I also discovered Berthold Meier's wry sense of humor. In his letter from Gurs dated August 3, 1941, he commented that it was Tisha B'Av, the sad Jewish holiday that commemorates the fall of the Temple in Jerusalem. *"A day which we celebrate here often..."* he muses. In the same letter, talking as usual about the shortage of food, he says, "I can starve well."

The ultimate, final, tragic irony of Berthold Meier's story is that shortly after the visa allowing him to come to America was finally issued by the U.S. government, Germany took over Vichy France and closed it off. Instead of traveling by boat to America to his son Arthur, Berthold Meier was doomed to travel by train to Drancy and then east to Maidanek/Sobibor on Transport 50, where, if he survived the train ride, he was gassed to death on his arrival in March, 1943.

In the last letter he ever wrote, the saddest letter I have ever read in my life, here is what the hero of my story, my dear

The Hero of the Story

grandfather, wrote to his son before he was put on the trains that took him to his death. This hero even managed to find a way to say goodbye.

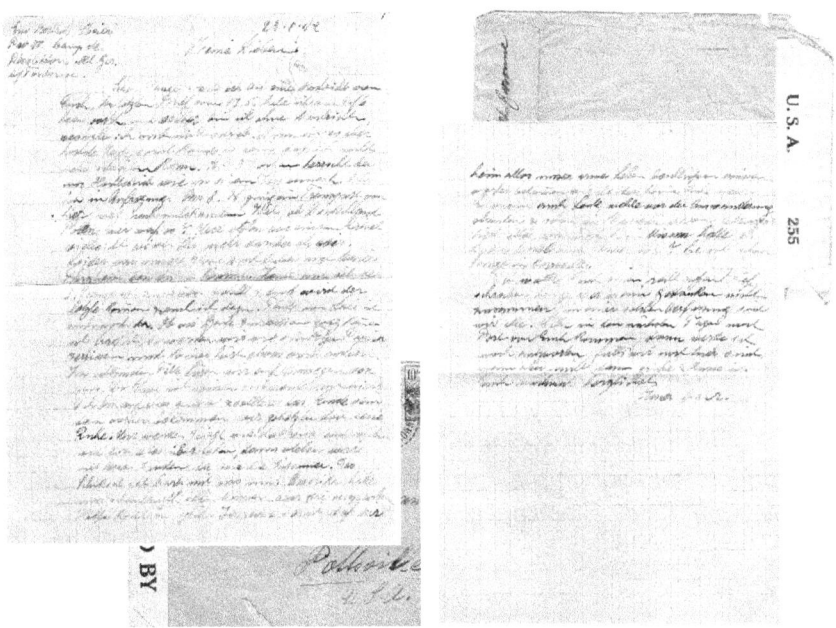

Berthold Meier
Pav. 80 Camp de Récébédou,
Ht. Gar. (=Haute Garonne) Toulouse
23.8.43

My dear ones!
   I've been waiting a long time for a message from you, I answered the last letter of May 17th on June 26th, and since then I've been without a message, which is why I didn't write either. But now it's high time, otherwise I might not be able to write anymore. For 3 weeks we have been busy as in a wasp's nest. Everything's in a state of excitement. On the 8th, a transport from here to an unknown destination went away, whether Germany, Poland, who knows? We're facing a mystery, maybe you know more about it than we do. Unfortunately, our Elise was there as well, also M. from Pforzheim, whom you know. Today the 3rd transport is put together & soon the last one will come

Chapter Forty-One

& I will join too. Aunt von Lahr's here, too. Whether we both get away together is questionable, so we are torn apart like a shred of paper, and no one hears anything from the other. In the worst case, we'll listen to detours. We don't know where Elise is today. I'm ready for anything & should it be the end because we rushed people don't get any rest before then. We are hunted like the game, and should we survive, we are left with empty hands like gypsies. Fate is tough on us. America could have helped us a long time ago, but the promised help is coming too late. I expect that we will have to decide our poor life without a home, but we will not be able to rest before then.

People who were about to emigrate and were already in Marseille, have been transported, everything that didn't have a visa. Whether Lydia Model was present or not? She's been in Marseille a long time.

I wanted to write you a rather good letter, but I can't put my thoughts together, we are all in bad shape. If there is any mail coming from you in the next few days, I will reply if we are still here, but if not, then I greet and kiss you once again heartily,

Your, Father

Do you see what I mean about Berthold Meier, my grandfather—the hero of my story?

Chapter Forty-Two
A Tragic Tale

I was almost finished with the first draft of my book, just filing documents in archival envelopes to keep busy during the Coronavirus Pandemic, when I found this postcard, which appeared to be written by two people. I didn't remember seeing it before, and I couldn't find it in my files on the computer, so I scanned it and sent it off to Martin, not knowing what a very tragic tale I was about to uncover.

Here is Martin's translation of the postcard, showing that it was indeed written by two people:

Chapter Forty-Two

Gengenbach 18. 7. 38

Dear Arthur! It is a special pleasure to send you for the first time heartfelt birthday wishes from your old home country across wide oceans. May happiness continue to be so dear to you. This is what your friend Ernst wishes you with all his heart.

Dear Arthur! Congratulations and wish you all the best. With longing we wait for your answer. Isn't it possible to find out if a guarantee is given or not? The uncertainty is unbearable. One does not make any further decisions.
Best regards, your Mrs. Fetterer

With the translation, however, Martin sent the following email:

Dear Susan,
Ernst Fetterer was the son of Anna Fetterer, where Berthold and Sophie had their last home. Ernst (born 1906) was 1938 in Dachau with Berthold, then deported from Stuttgart to Riga. Anna Fetterer and her sister were at Gurs but survived and lived after war in Strasbourg. I met her grandson Jules Levy, and he told me something about the family. He died meanwhile.

Fetterer was a name that rang a bell for several reasons. After my grandparents were forced by the Nazis to sell their house on Grünstraße in 1939, they moved into the Fetterer house, the *"Judenhaus,"* "Jew House," designed to house the Jews who were left in Gengenbach. This house on Market Square was Berthold and Sophie Meier's last home in their beloved town. It was from the Fetterer house that all the remaining Gengenbach Jews were taken by truck to Offenburg on October 22, 1940 on their journey to Gurs.
Then I remembered that I had also seen the name Fetterer in a letter from Jacques (Jakob) Valfer to my father, dated March 28, 1941, postmarked Leeds, England, in which he asks my father to write to his parents, now at Gurs, to inquire if Ernst Fetterer,

his cousin, is there at Gurs with them. He wasn't. Ernst had disappeared and no one knew what had happened to him.

Lastly, I went back and found a letter from Fritz Valfer written in 1954 to my mother after my father died, in which he spoke about my father and the Fetterer family. *At her house Arthur was like at home*, were his words, referring to the fact that it was Mrs. Fetterer, now living in Strasbourg, to whom he would have to tell the sad news of my father's death.

As I began to piece together the story about what happened to the Fetterer family, it was with a gradually dawning sense of horror that I began to understand that Ernst Fetterer, a friend who cared enough to send my father, now living in America, birthday wishes in July of 1938, had probably suffered the worst the fates could conjure up—tragic is too pale a word to use but it is all I can come up with.

Ernst was born in Schorndorf on March 4, 1906, but he grew up in Gengenbach where his widowed mother, Anna Valfer Fetterer, ran a textile shop in the Market Square with her sister and brother, Sophie and Ludwig Valfer. It was Ernst and his mother who wrote the two messages on the postcard.

Ernst with his cousins Jakob and Fritz Valfer in 1926

Ernst Fetterer in 1939

Chapter Forty-Two

Despite his mother's pleading for help to my father, Ernst did not get out of Germany. Along with my grandfather, his uncles Adolf, Isaak, and Ludwig Valfer, and his cousins, Jakob and Fritz Valfer, Ernst was sent to Dachau in 1938 after Kristallnacht. His brother-in-law, Fritz Levy, his sister Johanna's husband, was also sent to the camp.

After getting out of Dachau in January 1939, Ernst went to live with Johanna Levy, his sister, his brother-in-law Fritz, and their young son Jules in Pirmasens, near Stuttgart, where he became engaged to a girl. This is how he came to be in Stuttgart when the deportation from there occurred in December of 1941.

Jules Levy, Johanna and Fritz's son, was sent by his parents on March 5, 1939 to Limoges, in the south of France, to relatives named Falk with whom he spent the war. This saved Jules' life, and in 1946, he returned to Strasbourg where he found shelter in a home for the children of deported Jews. He also found his grandmother, Anna Fetterer and her sister, Sophie Valfer, who had also survived the war and their time at Camp de Gurs. The women ended up spending the rest of their lives in a retirement home in Strasbourg.

Jules lived until his death in 2016, in Haguenau, in North Alsace, France. He recalled the fun of visiting beautiful Gengenbach as a child, where he rode a "Dutchman," a special children's bike, around Market Square. He remembered his Uncle Ernst's red Zündappi motorcycle and his canoe for riding on the nearby Kinzig River.

Because he was in Stuttgart, instead of being sent to Gurs in France with the rest of his family from Gengenbach, Ernst ended up being transported from Stuttgart east to the Riga Ghetto on December 1, 1941.

I looked up deportations from Stuttgart to Riga and discovered this photograph, taken on December 1, 1941. When I discovered it, I was aghast at how closely it resembled my mental image of the Schillersaal in Offenburg on October 22, 1940, where my grandparents waited for the train to Gurs. Each time I see it, it is chilling for me to realize that Ernst Fetterer may very well be in this photograph!

A Tragic Tale

This photograph is from a film made in Stuttgart, Germany on December 1, 1941, by the Nazis who wanted to record their deportation activities

The difference between this deportation and the one in Offenburg is that there are many more people in this photograph than there were in Offenburg—by most accounts there are about 1000 here. Also, the people also are not headed for Gurs in France; they are headed in cattle cars to Riga, in what is today Latvia. Most of these men, women, and children were shot upon their arrival in Riga or put to deadly labor in the Ghetto. There were virtually no survivors.

Somehow, Ernst Fetterer managed to survive until August 10, 1944, when by then he was 38 years old. The records show that he was sent to the Stutthof Concentration Camp where he was no doubt put to death immediately. The information I found about life in the Riga Ghetto and the Stutthof Concentration Camp foretold a tragic ending for this dear friend of my father's.

The story of what happened to the people in the Stuttgart deportation picture, while different from what happened in Gurs in 1940, is another tragic example of the Nazis' attempt to make Germany *Judenrein*, Free of Jews.

Chapter Forty-Two

This paperwork shows the meticulous record-keeping by the Nazis for prisoner #2103455, Ernst Fetterer, at Stutthof Concentration Camp

Jules Levy completed this form in 1997 with information about the death of his uncle, Ernst Fetterer, to be recorded at Yad Vashem, the Holocaust memorial in Jerusalem

On a transport from Stuttgart on April 26, 1942, Johanna and Fritz Levy, Ernst's sister and brother-in-law, were sent to the Izbica Ghetto in German-occupied Poland where they both died.

Although Anna Fetterer survived Gurs and spent her later years in Strasbourg, France, it is haunting to contemplate how she may never have known what happened to her son or her daughter. Much of the information about the fate of the victims of the Nazis became known too late for many of the survivors of the Holocaust to have known about in their lifetimes.

Chapter Forty-Two

Uncovering the story of Ernst Fetterer made me realize something very ironically eerie.

As they all climbed into the Gestapo truck on Market Square in Gengenbach on their way to Gurs on October 22, 1940, at least my grandparents had the comfort of knowing that their son Arthur, my father, was safe and sound in Reading, Pennsylvania.

That is more than could be said for Anna Fetterer.

Chapter Forty-Three

An Unfortunate Coincidence

In August, 2021, I decided to look up my family on Ancestry.com to see if there was anything new to find that I didn't already know. I started by putting in the town, Gengenbach, and to my surprise, I discovered that someone else had also inquired about the town—a Barry Bloch from St. Louis. Bloch rang a bell—one of the other two Jewish children in my father's class in elementary school in Gengenbach was Paula Bloch.

I contacted Barry Bloch, and it turned out that he was Paula's nephew, her brother Gustav's son. Much to my delight, he had Jacques Valfer's daughter Marilyn's email address in England. And to my further surprise, when I wrote to Marilyn, she sent me her cousin Sylvia's information in Florida!

Sylvia was the daughter of the third Jewish child in my father's class, Fritz Valfer. Among the correspondence I had in my collection were letters from both Valfer men to my father, so their names were familiar to me. Fritz had settled in New York and Jacques in England. In fact, Fritz Valfer was the man who wrote a most poignant letter to my mother in 1954 after my father's death. In it, he mentions his daughter, Sylvia, then a young girl.

Eventually, Sylvia and I spoke on the phone. After talking to her, I realized how very much more I knew about the fate of my grandparents than she did about hers—thanks to Martin Ruch. The same was true for Marilyn, with whom I exchanged a number of emails. Sadly, she told me that her mother, Hedy Geismar, had just died a few weeks earlier. Her mother, she said, had never known where her father, Siegfried, had ended up after Gurs.

I let Martin know that I had met up with these three people.

To my surprise, a few days later, I got an email from him, telling me that Adolf Valfer, Sylvia's grandfather, had been on Transport 50 from Drancy to Maidanek with my grandfather. I emailed Sylvia and told her, including Marilyn in the email. I

Chapter Forty-Three

heard back from Marilyn, asking me to find out if Martin had any information as to the final whereabouts of her mother's father, Siegfried Geismar. So, I emailed Martin again and received an answer from him very quickly.

All three men, my grandfather, Berthold Meier, and Sylvia's grandfather, Adolf Valfer, born within weeks of each other in 1880 in Gengenbach, as well as Marilyn's grandfather, Siegfried Geismar from Offenburg, were sent to Drancy and put on Transport 50 to Maidanek/Sobibor. If any of them survived the ride he was gassed upon his arrival. It was too bad that we didn't connect sooner so her mother could have known about her father—not that it was good news.

Which brings me, in the end, to two dreadfully unfortunate questions:

- Was it of any comfort to these men to have old friends around them on their ride to hell?
- Is it of any comfort to Sylvia and Marilyn and me that we share this most unfortunate coincidence?

Sadly, I think the answer to both my questions is "no."

Chapter Forty-Four

How Was the Play, Mrs. Lincoln?

As far back in my life as I can remember, the pile of letters and postcards, written to my father, mostly in German, had been around—in the attic in Pottsville and in my mother's closets in Reading, Philadelphia, and Miami, until she finally handed them off to me about 20 years ago. For all that time, I had no idea what was in them until I found Dr. Martin Ruch. Sending the letters to him to translate, of course, would change my ignorance of knowing what they said.

After Adam and I scanned the letters and I began working with Martin, I could not imagine that the translations he sent me would be so excruciatingly painful to read. To hear the truth of what my grandparents were experiencing at Gurs from their own mouths was horrendous. I cannot even envision what it must have been like for my father to read those letters when they came in the mail from 1937 to 1943.

My mother lived until 2012—how I wish I had gotten the translations done while she was still alive. She would have been able to tell me how my father reacted when the letters from his parents arrived, one by one. He was desperately, but unsuccessfully, trying to get them visas, but they couldn't understand that. It is hard to image what those letters did to him.

Reading the December 28, 1940 article in the Philadelphia Record about Gurs that I found among his papers, I realized that my father knew what his parents were going through. So, by the way, did any other American reading the newspaper that day. The man I knew cared deeply about his parents—he was a devoted only child! He loved them very much. Getting and reading those letters and that newspaper article must have been overwhelming for him. However, I know that I will never have the answer to my question about how he handled it. That's the way it is. All I know is that the trauma and stress that began in 1933 did him in only twenty years later.

Chapter Forty-Four

Therefore, the biggest shock I have experienced over the last five years was coming to realize that not only did I lose my grandparents to the Holocaust—I lost my father too.

Just before Covid, I went to see the movie, *Operation: Finale,* the latest version of the capture of Adolf Eichmann in Argentina. There was a time when I could not have gone to see that movie. I would have run out of the theater ten minutes into it, crying hysterically. However, what has happened since my trip to Gurs has changed me forever—it still made me cry to see the actual pictures and footage of the Nazi's victims, especially the mothers with their children, but at the end of the movie, when they showed how Eichmann was convicted, hanged, cremated in an oven especially built to replicate the ovens used during the Shoah, and his ashes scattered in the ocean so he would never rest in peace, I felt joy. I wanted to stand up and cheer, but I didn't think the rest of the audience at the theater in South Miami would appreciate my sentiment. I did mentally cheer, through my tears, both his capture and death and my ability to watch the movie. After what I've learned from my research about the part Eichmann played in the fates of Berthold and Sophie Meier, despising him and watching how he died was very appropriate and long overdue. Managing to sit though that movie was a revelation to me—I had finally begun to deal with the truth.

Because of the miraculous chain of events that has occurred over the past six years, I finally found out many truths. Painful truths. And how do I feel now?

Now that I know what happened to my family, I take the Holocaust even more personally—deep down inside I still really believe that I escaped death only by being born a generation too late—that only good fortune kept me from being a witness to, or a victim of, the horrors that the Nazis brought to my family. And of course, I now also understand what an enormous influence the Holocaust had over my entire life, perhaps even to my genes, though I grew up in Pennsylvania, in the good old USA.

And what do I believe about the Third Reich and its ability to sweep the Meier family, Germans to the core, up in its monstrous rage? I understand now how the treatment of the Germans by the victors of WWI set the stage for the rise of the Nazis. Once in power, the Nazis and Hitler found it easy to find someone to blame for the price exacted from them: the Jews.

In my research, I found Theodore Herzl to have been a prescient prophet of doom with his prediction of what was coming in Europe—his was an accurate, dire vision of the coming Holocaust. Herzl posed the idea that the Jews were traditionally seen as disruptive immigrants, never belonging to any country in which they lived. He also advanced the fact that Jews were always seen as intolerable economic competitors since the beginning of time, no matter where they lived. Adolf Hitler called them "parasites." And finally, Herzl's view was that contemporary European Jews were now also seen as subversive radicals— and looking to the socialism that was developing in Russia and Eastern Europe at that time, certainly must have contributed to his thinking about the coming fate of the Jews. Herzl had a lot of ancient history under his belt to use as forewarning when he predicted the future—anti-Semitism was and still is the oldest form of prejudice that has ever existed in the world.

While, unfortunately, Herzl's reasoning clearly mirrors the justifications the Nazis used for the Holocaust, it doesn't really apply to the Meier family in their house on Grünstraße; I do not believe my family members were seen as outsiders, as economic threats, and certainly not as socialists either. I think they really had quietly blended into the village as middle-class Germans over a period of hundreds of years. Furthermore, Berthold Meier had shown his support for Germany by serving as a German soldier in WWI. I heard Rabbi Michael Berenbaum, a Holocaust scholar with the American Jewish University, say something that really struck a chord with me, "The pessimists left, and the optimists stayed." Maybe that is, curiously, what describes my grandparents. I believe that my grandfather still thought of himself as a German and longed to be back in his home in Gengenbach right up to the moment he went to the ovens at Maidanek or Sobibor.

Chapter Forty-Four

How then to explain what ultimately happened to them? In the end, I believe, what befell the Meier family was simply that they were Jewish, and the crimes their neighbors in Gengenbach committed, in many cases, were to just keep silent and stay out of trouble with the Nazis. The conspiracy theories about the Jews that the Nazis promoted worked so well that they were able to take over power and exterminate millions of people, while much of the world looked on, silently.

Sadly, I believe it *could* happen again—how could I know what I have learned in life and especially in the last twenty years and not think that? The dark side of me still suffers from a lack of feeling safe, of fear, that many of my Jewish American friends don't have and can't understand.

Many American Jews I know mirror my father and his parents, who surely thought of themselves as Germans first, then Jews. That does not differ from what most American Jews think about themselves today. *After all, they are Americans!* The Meier family probably could never have anticipated that in the first months of 1933, once Hitler took over the government, the Jews of Germany would become outsiders very quickly. I try to imagine what that was like for my father, and even though I have read many accounts of how drastically life changed for him, I still have trouble imagining what he felt. How I wish I could have asked him what it was like for him.

That probably makes this memoir a cautionary tale, particularly at this moment in time. I try hard not to confuse 2023 with 1933, but the rise of nationalism, White Supremacy, multiple conspiracy theories, and of course, anti-Semitism in all its ancient forms and in its newest form—anti-Zionism, make me feel horribly insecure. What is happening makes me very concerned. As I watch with horror the huge increase in anti-Semitism in America, listen to the news about anti-Zionism on college campuses, watch the marching and singing of "Jews will not replace us!" in Charlottesville, and see the ongoing threats to Jews and Jewish institutions that I witness all around me, I am reminded of what my father saw in Nazi Germany in 1933. The uptick of hatred for the Jews I hear on social platforms is once again the repetition of the same old scary tropes of blaming the Jews for everything that goes back a thousand or more years. The problem is so extreme that the State Department now has a special envoy to monitor and combat anti-Semitism, Ambassador Deborah Lipstadt.

CNN's Wolf Blitzer's program Never Again about the Holocaust Museum in Washington made me sit and sob as I watched it. So did the Ken Burns' series The U.S. and the Holocaust. These programs were dreadfully personal for me.

On the other side of the story, it is not all darkness for me. There is the incredibly unexpected bonus that has occurred since Martin Ruch translated the letters. It is that I have come to know and love my grandparents and to consider them a part of my life. It is very hard to love people you have never known, but now I feel like I have met Sophie and Berthold Meier. They have moved out of the green photo album and into my life! Reading their letters has made them come alive. Their very distinctive personalities came through in their writing. They even scolded my father just as I scolded my own son. They are real people to me now and I love them.

Chapter Forty-Four

My grandparents' names on the Holocaust Memorial in Miami Beach, Florida

I also found my father, even though I did not know I was looking for him! While doing my research and reading all the letters, I was shocked to discover how many drastic changes and losses the man who was my father lived through in his short life of 43 years. It surprises me that I never got a sense of hopelessness from him—he went on enjoying life in a positive way and encouraging me to do the same until the day he died. I have come to respect his resiliency and to be deeply grateful that he passed it on to me.

But I think he kidded himself about his own temperament. In a letter he wrote to my mother in 1945, while he was in the Army, he said, speaking of a man he knew who had just died very young, *"Take a lesson to take things easy and not to worry. Then you live longer and better. I think easy-going people never die of heart failure."* He was cautioning her not to worry so much—something he had been saying to her since he met her. She *was* a worrier! If I could, I would say, "Well, Daddy, I don't think *you* were as easy-going as *you* thought you were, and *I* don't think *I* am either. I believe I got your creative energy along with your positive view of life and your resilience. And your high blood pressure..." If I could talk to him today, I would tell him that I believe what he lived through during the Holocaust killed him when he was far too young.

Learning what my father experienced before he left Germany has been one of the ghastliest things I have had to deal with as I did my research and wrote my book. Discovering how much frustration and stress he went through dealing with what befell his parents, family, and friends, and understanding that the effect on him from all of this led to his early heart condition and his premature death at age 43 has been very painful to understand and accept.

I am still trying to digest it.

And, finally, the biggest surprise of all is that in writing this book, I discovered myself! All those losses, so early on, subconsciously informed my thoughts and behavior all through my life. No wonder I became an overachiever. It turned out that I was achieving for four people, three of whom had died prematurely. I never understood why I always felt such an urgent need to succeed! Now I do. After all, my father did tell me on my 2nd birthday to be *successful* in a *long, great life*! I have worked very hard to make up for all that was lost without knowing I felt the need to do so. Maybe now I can relax...

The words of Hortense Calisher, in her short story, <u>The Middle Drawer</u>, express what I think about myself and my life. *"Death, she thought, absolves equally...but never the living...The living carry, she thought, perhaps not one tangible wound but the burden of the innumerable small cicatrices imposed on us by our beginnings; we carry them with us always, and from these, from this agony, we are not absolved."*

The circle has finally closed, almost ninety years after it was torn open. The missing layers of generations of my family have been found, but closure won't make anybody happy. It won't make up for what happened. It won't bring with it any relief from the pain of the Holocaust and my family's terrible deaths.

Chapter Forty-Four

It won't change the fact that my brother, my son, and I are the end of the Meier family. But at least the truth will finally be acknowledged. Now there is nothing left to do but share their story.

Never forget. We must become the voice of those who have been silenced.

Serendipity.

Epilogue

I was intrigued to learn recently that there is a fairly new field of science called Behavioral Epigenetics. It is based on the premise that traumatic experiences in our past, or a recent ancestor's past, can leave molecular scars that adhere to the DNA inside the neurons in our brain, resulting in a biological memory of what the ancestor experienced.

The main finding from the research which I find most relevant is called "transgenerational trauma transmission," which addresses the possibility that a child or grandchild of a Holocaust victim might suffer from a greater vulnerability to stress, predisposing them to anxiety disorders such as PTSD.

The study shows that in other descendants, ironically, the opposite can occur: some offspring of Holocaust victims might have greater resiliency. Epigenetics adds a new psychological dimension to heredity and environmental factors, suggesting an effect of the transmission of trauma on and to the nervous system.

Some of the research in America and Israel is being done on the descendants of people who survived the Holocaust to see if, perhaps, they have different stress hormone profiles than their peers.

I was bemused to read that trauma transmission often leads to the writing of memoirs! To which I will add my own words of caution—write at your own peril! This memoir took six long years to write...and if someone doesn't take it out of my hands, I may go on revising it forever...SMMK

Acknowledgements

I am very thankful to my dear father for leaving me with such joyous memories even though we had only eleven brief years to create them. I am grateful that he passed on his resilience to me; it sure has come in handy over the last 81 years. As I reread his letters to my mother while I was doing my research, I was astounded at what a good writer he was, especially given that English was his third language. Perhaps my love of writing also came from him. Finally, the mantra he taught me that "all roads lead to Rome," has supported me throughout my entire life, not just on road trips.

Thank heavens my dear mother lovingly and respectfully schlepped around all of my father's possessions after he died. Without all that stuff, especially the letters and photo album, I never would have had the resources I needed to write my book. I wish she were around to see what I created from them.

My love and thanks to Franz Blum, may he rest in peace, for keeping me connected to Gengenbach after my father's death and for his help in arranging for Elfriede and Adolf Lohmüller's guidance during my 1968 visit to Gengenbach. As research over time began to reveal what had really happened during the Holocaust, Franz supplied me with the latest information. He would be delighted to know that I finally left my *Cave of Avoidance* and wrote this book. His wish that I remember my father and their beloved home—Gengenbach—certainly has become a reality. How I wish you could read this, Franz.

My son Adam was the first person who tried to write the story of the ring in the cookie for a creative writing class in high school. From the day I started writing, Adam encouraged me to keep working on this book. His input was always thoughtful and tremendously helpful.

Acknowledgements

He went to Germany with me in 2018, and I will never forget him on his hands and knees trying to polish the *Stolpersteine* in Gengenbach before the rededication ceremony. A can of Brasso sure would have been welcome! Adam's belief that I could really create this book gave me the courage to make it happen. His multiple readings of my various drafts and his wonderful suggestions have been so consistent throughout the years. Thank you, my dear son!

Both of my husbands, Lawrie Moss and Irwin Katz, helped me to have the experiences that inspired this book. Having them at my side made my research voyages very meaningful.

Lawrie encouraged me to visit Germany when Franz Blum told me to go to Gengenbach in 1968. As a result, I got to meet the people who had been so important in my father's life, especially Helmut Breunig, my father's best friend. Helmut would be so amazed and delighted to hear about the *Stolpersteine* and this book. Putting my grandparents' names on the wall of the Holocaust Memorial on Miami Beach was also truly a very special gift to me from Lawrie.

Thirty-two years later, in 2000, Irwin's planning helped to make the difficult trip to Camp de Gurs a reality, and he was always reassuring when I doubted that I would find Sophie Meier's grave. His empathy and patience with me during the two days we spent at Gurs was truly remarkable.

My thanks to the grandmother from Paris with the little black phonebook and to Serge Klarsfeld who said, "Madame Katz, if you think your grandmother is buried at Gurs, go. You will find her!" It was at Gurs that I woke up to the fact that I really did have a set of grandparents whose lives and deaths were a story I finally wanted to discover and write about.

Acknowledgements

My dear friend, Margot Berman, of blessed memory, was the only person I knew who had actually been imprisoned at Gurs. Margot, the creator of the wonderful library at Temple Beth Am, became my friend in the early 1970s. When I discovered the paper heart made by the schoolchildren of Gurs, I wanted to show it to her, but, of course, I couldn't. It was too late. It was strange for me to imagine that Margot could have been one of the children who actually made the heart that my grandmother received at Gurs on Mother's Day in 1941.

I wish I knew the name of the Viking Cruises' tour guide in Regensburg who told me about Gunther Demnig when I saw my first *Stolpersteine* on the tour she was leading. Wouldn't she be surprised to know how important a role she played in the writing of this book!

Speaking of Regensburg, it came as a surprise to me to learn that my Beth Am Rabbi, Rachel Greengrass, also had a connection to Regensburg. After the war ended, a group of former Bergen Belsen/Auschwitz Concentration Camp inmates, now displaced persons, were sent to Regensburg to live, including during the years 1945 and 1946. Among these Jews were her grandparents, Isaak and Fryda Grungrass. Rabbi Greengrass shared her grandparents' identity papers and photographs with me, which described their right to live in what appeared to be a close-knit, small Jewish community and even to drive cars.

Without the best email I ever got in my life, from Gerda-Marie Lüttgen, this adventure would never have begun! I will always be grateful to Gerda-Marie for connecting me to Dr. Martin Ruch and to the book he wrote that led to the school's *Stolpersteine* project in 2009. It was so special to have her at the rededication in 2018. I will also always remember the heavenly visit

Acknowledgements

I had with her and her dear late husband, Franz, at their home in Offenburg several days later.

Martin Ruch has made it his life's work to be the voice of those who have been silenced. Dr. Ruch's book about the Jews of Gengenbach led to the placing of my grandparents' *Stolpersteine* in front of their house. He has also made it his life's work to help the surviving members of the Jewish families of the Ortenau Region of Baden, Germany learn about how their ancestors lived and died. He honors the memories of those who perished in the Holocaust in a truly remarkable way, by teaching the younger generation of German youth their history. His interest in the Meier family, his dedicated hours of work translating all those letters, and his help in finding documents that helped me to tell the story, were a labor of love. A friend like Martin is truly a rare gift, which is why this book is dedicated to him. Thank you Martin, from the bottom of my heart, for helping me to become the voice of the Meier family.

My grateful thanks go to the administration, faculty, and students of the Marta-Schanzenbach-Gymnasium, whose project of dedicating the beautiful *Stolpersteine* in front of my grandparents' house in Gengenbach in 2009 was so special. Their willingness to rededicate them for Jeffrey, Adam, and me again in 2018 meant so much to us, the last members of the Meier family. Their work of creating many beautiful memorials to the Jews of their village who died in the Holocaust is truly a labor of love. Aiko Schuhmann, the Vice-Chancellor of the school, was instrumental in planning the rededication of the *Stolpersteine* for us. Some of the original project leaders, such as Peter Bechtold and Klaus Brenner, along with a student leader, Lucas Bechtold, helped to plan the important program for our memorable day.

Without the support of the city administrators

of Gengenbach for the dedication of the Meier Stolpersteine in 2009 and for the rededication of them in 2018, these memorials to the Jews of their village would never have happened. Many thanks to the current and past Burgermëisters, Thorsten Erny and Michael Roschach, and to the Head of the Bürgerservice, Michael Götz. The city officials supported the school projects in the past and still do, requiring courage and a commitment that I truly recognize and appreciate.

The day my brother, son, and I spent at the Schiller School in Offenburg in 2018 contributed a great deal to the writing of this book. My research had led me to understand that my father attended elementary school in his village of Gengenbach, but when he graduated, he moved on to finish his high school education at the Oberrealschule, now the Schiller-Gymnasium in Offenburg, the only Jewish boy from Gengenbach to do that. I also came to recognize that there are many pictures of him at the school in the green photo album. When I planned our trip to Germany to rededicate the *Stolpersteine*, Martin Ruch arranged with Alois Lienhard, the former vice-principal of the school, for us to visit the school my father graduated from in 1930. I received a lovely letter from Dr. Christina Schmitt, the Head of the History Department, inviting me to meet and speak to some of the students who knew both the history of the Holocaust and also spoke English. Talking with those students was a treat for this old schoolteacher.

What I did not realize ahead of time was that this was the first chance that Jeffrey, Adam, and I had to literally walk in Arthur Meier's footsteps, to walk through the halls of the school where he had walked, and finally, to stand in the same place where he stood in the photograph I had looked at for 80 years in the green photo album. It made our father seem real to Jeffrey

Acknowledgements

and me, his children, who had lost him in 1954, and for Adam, his grandson, who never met him. I am grateful to Martin Ruch for arranging the visit and to Manfred Keller, the Head of Schiller, for welcoming us back as though inviting us into a time machine to revisit the past.

I dreaded seeing the gymnasium of the school in Offenburg where my grandparents had spent their last hours in Germany waiting for the train to Gurs. Setting foot in that room was one of the most difficult things I have ever done in my life. The fact that the teachers and students of the school remember that day every single year is truly a tribute to the fact that there are still remarkably good people who live in Germany and that I was lucky enough to have the opportunity to meet some of them.

Meeting Annemie Sewald, the last person left on Earth who knew Berthold Meier, offered us the opportunity to walk in different footsteps this time, those of our grandfather, Berthold Meier. Even if Annemie did not remember why we were bringing her bonbons, her serendipitous accidental appearance in my book in Chapter 17 as the little girl who watched the Jews being loaded onto trucks, headed for Gurs, still gives me goosebumps to contemplate!

I was given the gift of encountering a series of people who supplied me with the facts that allowed me to follow the trail of information which ultimately led to the writing of this book. Sadly, this gift was not given to everyone. First cousins, Marilyn Valfer Jaffa and Sylvia Valfer Levy, the children of my father's Jewish contemporaries from Gengenbach, did not have the extraordinary luck that I did in finding out exactly what happened to all of their family members. The fates tragically contrived that many losses were shared by

Meier and Valfer family members, weaving our stories together. Therefore, I lovingly gift this book to Marilyn and Sylvia and to the few other surviving members of the Jewish families of Gengenbach. It is their story, too.

I am hugely thankful to the many people who helped to make the actual writing of this memoir, in many drafts, possible. Without their help, my dream of creating this book would never have come true.

I quickly realized as I began, with Martin's help, to glue together the historical facts that I needed to know in order to write about the Holocaust, that I had a very shallow understanding of what had really happened—what happened in the years that led to the Holocaust, what happened from 1933 on in Germany and elsewhere, and what gave the Nazis the power to achieve their terrible goals? I turned to <u>Why? Explaining the Holocaust</u>, the book by Dr. Peter Hayes that I read about in the New York Times and that had just been published in 2017. What an education I got. I digested the book from cover to cover and even asked questions of Dr. Hayes by email. His history of the Holocaust gave me a foundation on which to place the facts I was discovering in my research. It gave me a context in which to place the information Martin Ruch was giving me about what happened to my family and the other residents of Gengenbach. Dr. Hayes' book was truly the scaffolding that allowed me to tell my family's story in an historically accurate fashion. My tattered copy, filled with post-it notes, is a testimony to how valuable his book really was to me! I was glad to see that Peter Hayes spoke several times in Ken Burns' special on PBS about immigration to America. What a wonderful teacher he is.

My cousins Bobby and Joyce are the only family members left who remember my father's entry into the

Acknowledgements

Wise family. Joyce remembered my parents' wedding and was able to supply some other family facts. Bobby remembered some scary interesting facts about the Nazi sympathizers and supporters from Wyomissing, PA and how they showed their support of Hitler, such as the huge swastika painted on the side of the Wyomissing fire station!

I am grateful to Rabbi Alan Weitzman who believed that I could write this book long before I did. He was the one who encouraged me to begin the work with Martin Ruch. He would be so proud at what I have managed to accomplish—rest in peace my dear friend.

When I first started writing my memoir, I was a student at OLLI at the University of Miami. I want to thank my teachers Eric Selby and George Wendell and my fellow students for their encouragement at helping me figure out what I was trying to write in my early, bumbling attempts. Looking back, I realize how patient they were with me and my indecision about what I was doing then. They will have to see what I achieved in the end to believe it.

The late Rita Steinhardt Botwinick, Ph.D., a professor at UM, taught me some interesting facts about the Holocaust and served as an inspiration when I read her memoir, Gratefully Yours.

I've known for many years that if I ever got around to writing a book about my grandparents, I wanted to call it A Shortage of Grandparents. I first read those words "...there was a severe shortage of grandparents after the war. Actually, there weren't that many available uncles, aunts, nephews, nieces, or cousins, either..." in Thane Rosenbaum's book Second Hand Smoke. I was astounded to realize that in his book, Thane had just described my childhood when it came to my father's side of the family. I had never thought about it, but it was absolutely true. I had absolutely no family on the Meier-Roland side!

Acknowledgements

When I contacted Thane Rosenbaum in 2000 and he agreed to let me use the lines from his novel for the title, I was thrilled. It was the perfect name for my book, especially since Thane and I apparently write from the same motivation—to bring to life what we can only imagine.

When I finished the first draft of my book, I gave it to several friends to read. I told them to be honest—that I welcomed their reactions and suggestions.

My first reader was Susan Fletcher. Susan has stuck with me throughout the whole process—what a dear friend she is! We have been friends for so long that she remembered the window shades in my classroom at Beth Am and reminded me about them.

My next two readers were Joan Fisher and Jennifer Resnick. All of my readers came up with wonderful observations that I accepted, gladly. Their willingness to read my rough, clumsy attempt at a first draft and to share their creative ideas made an enormous difference as they helped me to write the memoir that exists today. Their positive attitudes toward what I was doing meant a great deal to me at a time when I desperately needed that support. When they read it, I hope they see how their ideas contributed to my finished book.

Phyllis Greenberg, my learned history teacher friend, read my next draft. With her sharp eyes, she picked up the fact that during the years of my writing, the expression "Holocaust Denial," which I had used several times in my book when referring to my inability to deal with the facts about the Holocaust, had become a truly pejorative term and needed to go! Phyllis also made many other wonderful suggestions that I gratefully took.

My beautiful book cover was created by the artist, Wendy Kornfield. I told Wendy what I was hoping for, and magically there it was—just what I had imagined! What a talented artist Wendy is, as you can see in the

Acknowledgements

watercolor painting of Gengenbach, Germany that appears on the back flap of my hardcover book. She painted it as a gift to me after my trip to my father's village in 2018. I am lucky to have her as a dear friend.

What can I say about my college friend Ellen Quietmeyer Morrow and her proofreading and editing skills? Ellen and I met in the registration line at West Chester University on the first day of our freshman year of college when she loaned me $1. Sixty-three years later, Ellen applied her incredible proofreading and editing skills to what I thought was my perfect, finished book, but turned out to need a lot of fixing. Ellen's patience and perseverance is astounding. Thank you, dear friend, for your help back in 1960 and again in 2023. Apparently, it was serendipity that Meier and Quietmeyer met that day in the registration line!

Speaking of old friends—it was my friend of 70 years, Sonia Samet Ciflik, who found Mazo Publishers for me. Sonia was born in Poland, survived the Holocaust, grew up with me in Reading, PA, and ended up living in Safed, Israel.

Chaim Mazo, my publisher, was born in Jacksonville, FL and ended up living in Israel and publishing books there. Chaim's patience, persistence, and skills were exactly what I needed to publish my very unusual memoir. I am very grateful to him for helping to make this book possible.

Last, but certainly not least, I want to thank all of the students—hundreds of children over the years—that I worked with in my years as an educator, urging them to become writers. I realize now that all those girls and boys who took chances as they wrote their stories had quietly served as role models for me. Often discouraged, frequently frustrated, they plowed on, drafting, revising, sharing, and editing, until they got to publishing. Now I know how you all felt at the publishing parties where you courageously read your work to your fellow students or to your parents. Thank you for teaching me to be brave enough to follow in your footsteps!

I suspect that there may be names missing from my acknowledgements. Having imagined writing this book for most of my life, I probably had encouragement from people whose influence I can't remember. Please forgive me if you're one of them!

Sources

This memoir tells as accurately as possible the story of the impact of the Holocaust on the Meier family of Gengenbach, Germany. The recollections in the book are based on letters and postcards, official documents, photographs, anecdotes, quotes, inspirational newspaper articles, movies, television specials based on historical events, and in some cases, on fictional stories. Much of the material belongs to my family. However, through my many years of research, I have been inspired by and drawn information from many relevant sources. Whenever possible, I want to give credit to these enormously helpful people and resources.

Books, Articles, Documents, and Photographs

Angelos, James, *The New German Anti-Semitism*, (New York Times, May 21, 2019).

Botwinick, Rita Steinhardt Botwinick, PhD, *Gratefully Yours-From Nazi Untermensch to a Patch in the Rose Garden: A Historic Memoir*, (Teneo Press, 2015).

Calisher, Hortense, *The Middle Drawer*, (The New Yorker, July, 1948).

Diersburg: The History of a Jewish Rural Community 1738-1940, (Haigerloch, 2000).

Dzialoszynski, Samuel and Ruch, Martin, *Der Gute Ort: Der Jüdische Friedhof in Offenburg*, (Historymarketing.de, 2000).

Fink, Joanne, *Never Forget: We Must Become the Voice of Those Who Have Been Silenced*, (Zenspirations, 2018).

Frank, Werner L., *The Curse of Gurs: Way Station to Auschwitz*, (2012).

Gabi Aubele, *Jüdische Mitbürger in Gengenbach Während Der Zeit Des Nationalsozialismus*, (Lions International, November 1985).

Sources

Goldsmith, Martin, *A True Story of Music and Love in Nazi Germany: The Inextinguishable Symphony*, (John Wiley & Sons, Inc., 2000).

Hayes, Peter, *Why? Explaining the Holocaust*, (W. W. Norton & Company, 2017).

Klemperer, Victor, *I Will Bear Witness 1933-1941: A Diary of the Nazi Years*, (The Modern Library, 1999).

Laharie, Claude, *Le Camp de Gurs: 1939-1945 un aspect méconnu de l'histoire de Vichy*, (J&D Editions, 1984).

Mendelsohn, Daniel, *Before the Holocaust Fades Away,* (New York Times Magazine, July 14, 2002).

Niemals einen Schlussstrich: Jüdische Nachfahren der Gengenbacher Familie Berthold und Sophie Meier aus USA angereist, (Gengenbach Und Umgeburg, Mittelbadische Presse, Offenburger Tageblatt, Dienstag, 19, Juni 2018).

Roosevelt, Eleanor, *You Learn by Living: Eleven Keys for a More Fulfilling Life*, (Harper & Brothers Publishers, 1960).

Rosenbaum, Thane, *Second Hand Smoke*, (St. Martin's Press, 1999).

Ruch, Martin, *700 Jahre Geschichte der Junden in Gengenbach*: 1308-2008, (KulturAgentur, Willstätt, 2008).

Ruch, Martin, *Der Salmen: Geschichte der Offenburger Synagoge*, (KulturAgentur, Offenburg, 2002).

Ruch, Martin, *Gengenbach: Ein Stadtrundgang,* (A. Reiff GmbH & Cie. KG, Offenburg, 2006).

Ruch, Martin (Translator), *Susan Meier Katz, Florida, An Die Leser Der Gengenbacher Blätter*, (Gengenbach Blätter, 2019).

Ruch, Martin and Mendelsson, Eva, *Sylvia Cohn (1904-1942): Poems and Letters*, (KulturAgentur, Offenburg, 2022).

Ruch, Martin, *Zu Besuch in Der Alten Heimat: Familie Meier Kehrt Zurück,* (Gengenbach Blätter, 2018).

The Kinzig Messenger, (Gengenbach, Germany, 1919-1920).

United States Lines, *S.S. President Roosevelt*, (1937).

Vormeier, Barbara, *The Deportation of German and Austrian Jews From France 1942-1944*, (Éditions "La Solidarité," 1980).

United States Holocaust Museum, Washington, D.C.

Wiesenthal, Simon, *The Sunflower*, (Schocken Books, 1969).

Yad Vashem Holocaust Museum, Jerusalem, Israel.

Television Specials

Never Again: *The United States Holocaust Memorial Museum – A Tour with Wolf Blitzer,* Written by Will Cadigan, Directed by Mwita Chacha, (CNN, 2022).

The U.S. and the Holocaust, Written by Geoffrey C. Ward, Directed by Ken Burns, Lynn Novick, and Sarah Botstein, (PBS, 2022).

Movies

Operation Finale, Screenplay by Matthew Orton, Directed by Chris Weitz, (Metro-Goldwyn-Mayer and Annapuma Pictures, 2018).

The Last Suit, Written and Directed by Pablo Solarz, (Outsider Pictures, 2017).

About the Author

Susan Meier Moss Katz was born and grew up in what she calls the "Reading Railroad" area of Pennsylvania. In her late 20's, with her husband and son, she moved to Miami, Florida, where she has since lived for over 50 years. She holds a Bachelor of Science in Education degree from West Chester University and a Master of Science in Educational Leadership degree from Barry University.

Susan taught elementary education in public schools for six years and then for 22 years at Temple Beth Am Day School, where she also served as the Curriculum Coordinator and the Director of the Writing Program. In 1994, she became the founding Head of the Gordon Day School at Beth David Congregation. In 2001, she became the Director of Academics at St. Thomas Episcopal Parish School, where she worked for 12 years until her retirement in 2013. Children's writing was always her passion, and she founded writing programs in four elementary schools in Miami.

The author has a son Adam from her marriage to her first husband, Lawrence Moss, and two step-daughters, Laura (Brian Weissbart) and Paige, from her marriage to her late second husband, Irwin Katz. She has two grandchildren, Sydney Katz and Tucker Weissbart.

Susan has many hobbies; a visit to her home would reveal her love of collecting—from pink house paintings to shoes. Her most prized collection, perfectly fitting for a schoolteacher, consists of hundreds of apples, many received as gifts—from a handmade clay apple made for her many years ago by one of her former students and his grandmother to a Lalique crystal apple her dear friend Mimi gave her.

Susan also enjoys reading and traveling. She is still surprised at a series of events encountered on some of her trips, that led her, as though down an unseen, unknown path, guided by a series of unforeseen people and events, to have the experiences that allowed her to write this book.

www.ingramcontent.com/pod-product-compliance
Lightning Source LLC
Chambersburg PA
CBHW070540160426
43199CB00014B/2311